"Karen provides emotional insights and spi[...] challenging moments when we question con[...] She points us to solid anchors that will hold us [...].

> —**Anita Agers Brooks,** inspirational business/life coach, common trauma expert, and author of Readers' Favorite International Book Award winner, *Getting Through What You Can't Get Over*

"As a woman who has been where so many lost, confused, and hungry Christians are in these troubled times, Karen is a trustworthy guide for those who wish to discover the will of God for their lives in the beautiful and sometimes painful narratives of their faith."

> —**Dr. Charles M. Anderson,** Dept. of Rhetoric and Writing, University of Arkansas at Little Rock

"After reading this book I felt like I had been with a childhood friend; the kind of friend you know everything about and who knows everything about you. Karen is an excellent writer and storyteller, but it's her vulnerability that makes this book so unique. This book felt like a Christian SparkNotes on the topic of women and worry."

> —**Lucille Zimmerman,** licensed professional counselor and author of *Renewed*

"Karen will guide you on how to commune with God and how to overcome the fear and unbelief that cripples so many Christians. Discover God's peace and REST through this journey of true life experiences seen through the lens of Scripture."

> —**Mike Huckabee,** former Governor of Arkansas

"Karen Jordan will change your thinking and your heart. She skillfully shows how to recognize the 'Red Flags' of negative self-talk and helps us speak Grace-talk as we walk with God through his Word. Karen's encouragement and vulnerability in sharing her stories reveals we are not in the battle alone. You will be grateful you joined this journey."

> —**Dr. Rodney Coe,** pastor, author of *The Rise of the Prophet*, and founder of liftupyourday.com

"Karen Jordan knows that words can change everything because she has experienced the power of God's life-changing Word in her own life. In this book, you will discover the elements of powerful prayer, purposeful faith, and a close walk with God."

> —**Debbie Moore,** Women's Missions Discipleship Consultant, Arkansas Baptist State Convention

"Karen not only identifies the problem of negative self-talk and the anxiety it produces, she also shares doable solutions. She connects with the reader on many levels because she has overcome this herself. Many lives will benefit from the wisdom found between the pages of this book."

> —**Linda Apple,** author and Arkansas regional speaker trainer for Stonecroft Ministries

"Karen shares her spiritual journey in a voice that is honest, unpretentious, and inspiring. You will be blessed by your encounter with her."

—**Dr. Sally Crisp,** Dept. of Rhetoric and Writing, University of Arkansas at Little Rock

"Drawing upon biblical truth that has taught her how to trust God for answers in life's 'waiting rooms,' Karen identifies red flags that might cause us to raise a *white flag* of despair. Then she offers original, easy-to-remember strategies such as 'Grace Talk' to help us learn to rest in God."

—**Carolyn Goss,** owner/partner of GoodEditors.com, co-author of multiple books, including *Equipped to Win,* as well as editor of numerous other works

"This book is a much-needed resource full of practical, biblical advice for any woman longing to win the spiritual battle over worry. By weaving her personal stories throughout the manuscript, Jordan comes alongside the reader as a fellow struggler, not an 'expert' who has it all together."

—**Dena Dyer,** professional speaker and musician, award-winning author of *Wounded Women of the Bible* and other books

"Karen has hit a grand-slam home run with *Words That Change Everything.* I will certainly encourage my clients/counselees to read this book. It's encouraging, inspirational, and instructional."

—**Dr. J. D. Stake,** LPC LMFT, retired Director of Counseling for the Arkansas Baptist State Convention

"As followers of Jesus, our new hearts long to follow our Savior obediently, and our sincere desire is that we would also be effective in prayer. With Karen's help, we can find confidence in both."

—**Shelley Hendrix,** author and speaker, founder of Church 4 Chicks

"For those who feel overwhelmed, exhausted, and weighed down by worries that so easily paralyze the soul, I encourage you to read this book and find the REST you have long desired in the comforting embrace of a Savior who invites you to cast all your worries on him and find peace."

—**Shawn Barnard,** lead pastor of Crossgate Church, author of The Tabernacle DVD study

"Karen encourages you to examine your life and know that God can set you free from the chains of negative thinking. This book will help you identify thoughts that cause worry or anxiety."

—**Andrea Lennon,** author and women's ministry speaker, True Vine Ministry, women's ministry specialist for the Arkansas Baptist State Convention

"Anger, fear, unbelief, anxiety—need relief from any of those? Find it here as Karen uses God's Word to guide us to solid answers for real issues. *Words That Change Everything* might just . . . well . . . *change everything!*"

—**Rhonda Rhea,** humor columnist, TV host, author of *How Many Lightbulbs Does It Take to Change a Person?*

WORDS THAT Change EVERYTHING

Speaking Truth to Your Soul

Karen Jordan

LEAFWOOD
PUBLISHERS

an imprint of Abilene Christian University Press

WORDS THAT CHANGE EVERYTHING
Speaking Truth to Your Soul

L E A F W O O D
P U B L I S H E R S
an imprint of Abilene Christian University Press

Copyright © 2016 by Karen Jordan

ISBN 978-0-89112-381-1

Printed in the United States of America

The author is represented by and this book is published in association with the literary agency of WordServe Literary Group, Ltd., www.wordserveliterary.com.

Cover design by ThinkPen Design, LLC
Interior text design by Sandy Armstrong, Strong Design

Leafwood Publishers is an imprint of Abilene Christian University Press
ACU Box 29138
Abilene, Texas 79699
1-877-816-4455
www.leafwoodpublishers.com

16 17 18 19 20 21 / 7 6 5 4 3 2 1

I'll write my story, Lord,

for all the world to see.

It's for your glory, Lord,

and not any of it for me.

I pray you'll guide me, Lord,

in every word I write.

And then just hide me, Lord,

and let them see your might.[1]

Not to us, Lord, not to us

but to your name be the glory,

because of your love and faithfulness.

(Ps. 115:1 NIV)

the Source of my inspiration, joy, peace, and REST.

[T]he Word

became human and made his home among us.

He was full of unfailing love and faithfulness.

And we have seen his glory,

the glory of the Father's one and only Son.

(John 1:14 NLT)

Acknowledgments

I thank my God every time I remember you. In all my prayers for all of you, I always pray with joy because of your partnership in the gospel from the first day until now. (Phil. 1:3–5 NIV)

My mother gave me a journal on my forty-fifth birthday and challenged me to list five things that I'm grateful for every day. I'm glad Mother only asked me to list five blessings a day, because it would be impossible to list all my blessings in one journal.

So how can I say thanks in one section of this book to all the people who have encouraged me in my writing life? Again, that might be an impossible task. But I want to mention a few of my faithful friends and family who have been a vital part of this particular book project.

To my tribe on Jordan's stormy banks. Dan, Adam, Tara, Jenni, Jonathan, Miles, Aidan, Ethan, Zach, Jill, Julia, and Ben—How could I have written this without your love, support, and willingness to let me share our family stories? Thank you. "Let this be written for a future generation, that a people not yet created may praise the Lord" (Ps. 102:18 NIV).

To my parents (in heaven). Gene Thomas Barnes Sr. and Burnelle "Nelle" (Allen) Barnes Baize—Thank you for the spiritual legacy of faith that you passed down to our family. And thank you both for giving me a glimpse of heaven as you crossed over to your promised land.

To my siblings and other family members. Tommy, Cathy, Leslea, Penny, Richard, Aunt Jo, Marilyn, Doug, and Mary—Thank you for allowing me to refer to you in this book. I'm so grateful for the prayerful support of my extended family who allowed me to share some of the most intimate and difficult seasons of our family's lives with the world.

To my brothers and sisters in Christ. Although I only mentioned a few of you by name in my book—Jack, Don, Shirley, Bibbie, Kathy, Sheila, Maxine, and Debbie—God has blessed me with a multitude of friends in the faith. I dare not try to list everyone who prayed for me—advising, listening, counseling, and consoling me through this long, drawn-out process. I pray God will give me the opportunity to thank you in person.

To my proofreaders for this project. Dan Jordan, Tara Ross, Anita Brooks, Kathryn Graves, and Mary Larmoyeux—Thank you for your honesty and your willingness to wield your red ink and offer your expert opinions during the entire writing process of this book. I'm blessed to be surrounded by such wonderful writers and editors.

To our WordServe team of agents and writers. My WordServe agent, Greg Johnson, and former WordServe agents, Alice Crider and Barbara Scott—Thank you for representing me and negotiating on my behalf during my journey to publication. I'm thankful to be part of the WordServe Literary Group, WordServe Water Cooler blog, and FaithHappenings.com.

To my Leafwood Publishing team. I'm honored to partner with you on *Words That Change Everything*. Thank you for your investment of time, resources, and hard work on this project. A special thanks to Mary Hardegree, Duane Anderson, and Seth Shaver at Abilene Christian University Press/Leafwood Publishing, Rachel Paul at Scribe Inc., and Sandy Armstrong at Strong Design.

To my other writing connections. God continues to bless me with many writing friends—the University of Arkansas at Little Rock (UALR), CLASSeminars, Little Rock American Christian Writers, Arkansas Women Bloggers, Arkansas Baptist News, Arkansas Baptist Minister's Wives blog, Hot Springs Village Writers Club, My Journey of Faith Ministries, StoryWriting Studio friends, and others who continue to offer their writing expertise and inspiration. I also appreciate my online mentor, Michael Hyatt (MichaelHyatt.com).

To my friends in ministry. Through the years, God has provided us with many wonderful faith connections around the world, from our homes in Arkansas and Texas. Over the past few years, I'm indebted to Crossgate Church of Hot Springs, the Summit Church of North Little Rock, Arkansas Baptist State Convention,

Stonecroft Ministries, and other church and faith groups who have supported me.

To my online inspiration. What would I do without my ongoing dose of inspiration from KLOVE.com radio and Brian Hardin of DailyAudioBible.com? May the Lord continue to bless your ministries as you lift up the Word of God.

To the Author and Finisher of my faith. Thank you, Jesus! "Therefore, since we are surrounded by such a great cloud of witnesses, let us throw off everything that hinders and the sin that so easily entangles. And let us run with perseverance the race marked out for us, fixing our eyes on Jesus, the pioneer and perfecter of faith" (Heb. 12:1–2 NIV).

Contents

Foreword

Introducing my wife Karen invites peril! Knowing my voice, my weaknesses, and my body language, she relies on her intuition like a mother with her firstborn child. She categorically rejects any pretentiousness, applause, embellishment, or exaggeration. She repels suggestions about success or failure, fame or fortune, and any hint that penning this book came from any source of inspiration other than the Lord. Expect to meet a woman honest with herself and others.

We grew up in the same small town, living in different worlds of faith, values, and religion when we were young. Unaware of Karen's immersion in Christianity, her traditional conservative church seemed unnatural to me, since my family did not attend church. Her parents would only allow me to date her if I attended their church services on Sundays and Wednesdays. I resisted their efforts at indoctrination, and I was always ready to debate their beliefs. But, unexpectedly, the power in scripture drew me, even if under mild duress. I feared their pastor and deacons! Instinctively, in their black suits and ties, they seemed to know that I did not know their God.

Facing matters of eternity, cultivating a relationship with Jesus Christ, and considering the possibility of missing heaven became reality for me. My relationship with Karen and her family caused me to be confronted by unknown holy concepts, such as sin, repentance, and the possibility of being spared from a place called hell.

We grew up quickly following our wedding. The challenges and frustrations of marriage, careers, and parenthood led us to painful places where we usually disagreed on everything. Then Christ saved us and propelled us on a new journey away from our hometown and families to attend seminary, following him to serve others.

Many somber days we battled over church, family, and finances. When both of our young children received bad news from our doctors—with debilitating health conditions demanding immediate treatment—stress, worry, and fear of the unknown hovered over our home. We had not anticipated threats to their lives when we moved our family to the seminary campus. We prayed together with other people of faith, and God responded to our circumstances and anxiety. God proved his concern and care for us in the miraculous ways he directed us during that season of life.

The years following our move to Arkansas demanded that we acclimate our faith to a different culture. We were confronted by beliefs and routines unlike what we experienced before. The expectations and demands of working for a denomination directed our faith walk and decided everything for us.

Where we worshipped, what we did after work, and our life routines were mapped out for us. Individual choices and the freedom to experience things outside of mainstream church life were abandoned. But when we stumbled headfirst into a painful family moral failure, God transformed us as we responded to his direction. Knowing God became Karen's only hope for sanity and reconciliation in the twisted wind of the crisis threatening to destroy our family.

We all survived, changed, and grew wiser from the storm. God's obvious hand on our family attracted many other parents to our door as he guided our steps in those puzzling days. They asked how we were able to endure and overcome the stress and shame. Our prayer life and response to the Word enabled us to live one day at a time, make difficult decisions, and thwart the devil's intentions to undermine our faith and witness to our community and extended family.

Many Christian women contacted Karen asking her to pray for them in the following years. They sought a friend who would respect their boundaries and honor their confidentiality. They needed a trustworthy mother who had overcome the storms of life that were presently battering their shorelines. Her prayers with them were intensely personal and heavy, and she learned to pass their burdens on to the Lord. At the time, I did not perceive the Lord preparing Karen for important new things. Her return to college, fulfilling the call on her life to write professionally, surprised me, even though I realized her intent was to give her all to him.

She loves to laugh but is sensible. Always concerned about others, she carries their burdens to the cross. Her family is always a priority, acknowledging her inability to shield them from the consequences of their unwise decisions. Instead, she chooses to intercede for them, leaning on the direction and inspiration of the Holy Spirit and her Bible for solutions. Karen prays for her children and grandchildren.

Karen shares her belief that God's written Word contains the power for emotional healing. It is revolutionary to those that receive it. She speaks of forgiveness as the first step for women to grow beyond their own boundaries of guilt, shame, and disappointments about their own past.

When I ask her to explain some of her thoughts, I know to expect the truth she has harvested from his Word. Weighed down by worry, she mined the Bible, seeking peace and rest. Harassed by humiliating memories and feelings of guilt and shame, she became relentless in rooting out what he had to say about forgiveness and repentance.

Go with her to the waiting rooms of life, where decisions are about life and death, both physical and spiritual. Find the remedy for your anxiety and unnatural fear. God's Word dispels unbelief and darkness surrounding those in deepest sorrow and doubt and impacts those seeking answers about how to live and reconcile their lives. His Word, speaking truth to your soul, will change everything!

—Dan Jordan

Preface

As I prepared to write this book, a sudden and disturbing vivid memory emerged from a time when I stepped out of my comfort zone to serve. I still feel the embarrassment of that day when I helped prepare the noon meal after a revival service in my hometown church.

A million doubts and fears raced through my mind that morning. *Was my skirt too short? Were my heels too high? Were my clothes too tight? Would someone ask me too much about my personal life? Why did I even come here in the first place?*

I would have preferred to hide in the church kitchen pantry as I stood in the serving line for our Southern-style meal—fried chicken, mashed potatoes, fresh vegetables, and rolls. My thoughts wandered back to the church nursery, hoping my son would be ready for a nap when we returned home. I knew I would need one.

I made my way to a chair at the end of one of the folding tables with the other "Baptist Young Women," trying to fit in the best way I knew how. I avoided eye contact with the evangelists and the church staff who sat facing us from their tables.

Since I was the youngest and newest member of the ladies' group helping that day, someone nominated me to pass out rolls to everyone. I tried to be a good sport, pretending to be pleased serving them. I forced a smile, left my seat, and strolled to the kitchen. I breathed a sigh of relief as the kitchen door closed behind me, away from the eyes of those gathered around the tables for lunch.

I stacked the rolls high on a large platter, hoping to avoid a second trip to the kitchen. I pushed the swinging door open with my back, clutching the serving plate with both hands. I had hoped to slip back into my seat and avoid being noticed or singled out again.

Then it happened. As I spun around, trying to balance myself with the huge platter of rolls, I tripped and fell to the floor, propelling everything across the room.

I can still recall everyone in the room gasping at the spectacle I had made of myself. Shame and embarrassment washed over me as I tried to look away from the snickers and whispers of the crowd. But I felt their piercing eyes fixed upon me. And I did not want to imagine how I must have looked to them, sprawled out on the floor with rolls and pieces of the shattered platter all around me.

Instead of lying there helpless like a squashed bug, I swallowed my pride, picked myself up, and asked, "Does anyone want another roll now?"

Several years later, after relocating to Arkansas, I visited a restaurant famous for their "thrown rolls." I wondered if they knew who first stumbled upon that idea.

As I wrote this book, my old fears and worries resurfaced, reminding me of that humiliating experience. *Do I dare expose more of my failures, worries, and vulnerability with an even larger audience? What if I make a total fool of myself again in front of my friends, family, and total strangers as they read some of my life stories?*

Then I remembered what I learned from my earlier failed attempt to serve others.

Forty years after I humiliated myself in my home church, the pastor's wife invited me to speak in that same fellowship hall at a Thanksgiving event sponsored by the women's ministry.

As I began to prepare my presentation, once again I recalled the first time someone asked me to serve at church. This time I was asked to share my stories—not to "throw rolls." But I still decided to share my humiliating story, revealing some of my own worries and vulnerability. God had given me an opportunity to overcome a moment of failure in the same context and venue, four decades later, as I stood on this promise from God's Word:

> "My grace is all you need. My power works best in weakness." So now I am glad to boast about my weaknesses, so that the power of Christ can work through me. That's why I take pleasure in my weaknesses, and in the insults, hardships, persecutions, and troubles that I suffer for Christ. For when I am weak, then I am strong. (2 Cor. 12:9–10 NLT)

I also believe in the power of story. When we share the stories that matter most, lives change and hearts heal. So, as you begin to read this book, I offer this confession:

> Here's a word you can take to heart and depend on: Jesus Christ came into the world to save sinners. I'm proof—Public Sinner Number One—of someone who could never have made it apart from sheer mercy. And now he shows me off—evidence of his endless patience—to those who are right on the edge of trusting him forever. (1 Tim. 1:15–16 *The Message*)

Words That Change Everything

Speaking God's Truth to Your Soul

Words are powerful; take them seriously. (Matt. 12:37 The Message*)*

I n recent years, everyone seems to be worried about something. We can't browse the Internet or turn on the TV news at night without being confronted with shocking stories. The media often provokes red flag emotional responses of worry, anxiety, fear, and panic with their sensationalized headlines, exaggerated news, and debilitating political gossip. And during our culture's most recent days, many of us have seen devastating events unfold in our own homes with our families.

A few years ago, it seemed as if I was camped in a hospital waiting room all the time. And the weight of the burdens inflicted a toxic toll on my health and attitude about life and the future.

Are you searching for an emergency exit to escape from a waiting room right now? Do you want to avoid wading through and enduring more of those same old sad stories? Do you want to forget about your own painful days? I do.

While drafting this book, I doubted my ability to deal with the subject of worry. I became exhausted just thinking about revealing my feelings. And exposing my dirty laundry in public seemed dangerous to me.

Yet I've learned crucial lessons in the waiting rooms of my life.

As I coped with my mother's impending death a few years ago, I searched for solace in every book I could find. And I discovered what I needed in God's Word. When all hope seemed lost, I adopted a powerful strategy for prayer and spiritual rest offered in the Bible:

> The Lord is near. Do not be anxious about anything, but in every situation, by prayer and petition, with thanksgiving, present your requests to God. And the peace of God, which transcends all understanding, will guard your hearts and your minds in Christ Jesus.
>
> Finally . . . sisters, whatever is true, whatever is noble, whatever is right, whatever is pure, whatever is lovely, whatever is admirable—if anything is excellent or praiseworthy—think about such things. Whatever you have learned or received or heard from me, or seen in me—put it into practice. And the God of peace will be with you. (Phil. 4:5–9 NIV)

Overview

Since most of life's waiting room experiences interweave both emotional highs and lows, I present *Words That Change Everything* in three distinct parts:

- *Part One—Red Flags.* Through personal stories and biblical application, this section suggests problem-solving strategies that can help you navigate negative self-talk and overwhelming worry. We will examine the red flags of worry and other crises of faith that can impact our lives. Plus, we will consider God's promises—*Words That Change Everything*—so you can begin *Speaking God's Truth to Your Soul*.

- *Part Two—REST.* These chapters present meaningful, true-life stories and suggest helpful ideas for managing your emotions based on Philippians 4:5–9. This passage tenders a strategic prayer plan for speaking truth and finding deliverance from worry, introducing the acronym REST—remember, exalt, surrender, trust.

- *Part Three—Retreat.* This last section offers real-life applications and introduces an additional prayer guide based on Lamentations 3:28–29: "When life is heavy and hard to take, go off by yourself. Enter the silence. Bow in prayer. Don't ask questions: Wait for hope to appear" (Lam. 3:28–29 *The Message*).

Why This Book

Write this down for the next generation so people not yet born will praise God. (Ps. 102:18 The Message)

I often feel compelled to share lessons as I'm learning them. So even as I battled with my own angst during turbulent times, I continued to research, write, and speak about what I came to understand about my emotions.

I resisted the idea of writing a book that focused on steps to overcoming worry, because my own emotional red flags still rippled overhead, warning me of potential harm. So I began to search for answers in my Bible. And as I focused on God's Word and gave my worries and concerns to him in prayer, his peace filled my heart and my mind as promised in Philippians 4:7.

I found God's peace during the dark and painful weeks when I was confined to intense waiting room environments. God proved faithful to his promises in each of those challenges, while giving me fresh hope and an expanded vision and plan for my future. Part of that plan involved sharing the lessons from the waiting rooms of my life with you. So thank you for allowing me to share what I've learned about the power of God's Word in *Words That Change Everything*.

Along my journey, each time I encountered other women who were distraught and worried, I wanted to encourage them with what I had discovered navigating my guilt-ridden emotions and negative self-talk. But all too often, the times and places where we crossed paths prevented any helpful dialogue.

I may have listened to your stories and prayed for you. At times, I might have even shared bits and pieces of my journey with you at church, school, or a writing conference. Perhaps we connected through a social network, or you noticed my stories in an online or printed publication. Today, I appreciate those avenues of publication because they enabled me to record my personal migration from worry and anxiety to "REST" and peace.

I still need a measure of God's Word every day as I wrestle to manage my reactions and responses to stress. Writing this book engaged the truths I embraced about responding to worry. But reading and speaking God's Word into my soul always helps me refocus my negative thoughts and overwhelming worries on eternal truths.

> Not that I have already obtained all this, or have already arrived at my goal . . . But one thing I do: Forgetting what is behind and straining toward what is ahead, I press on toward the goal to win the prize for which God has called me heavenward in Christ Jesus. (Phil. 3:12–14 NIV)

God's Word keeps my focus on his truth so I don't become distracted by negative thoughts that threaten my peace and rest. I continue to research, write, and teach on the subject because I know many women struggle with these same issues. So I'm compelled to record the lessons I've learned from the waiting rooms of my life. Plus, God's Word promises, "My grace is all you need. My power works best in weakness" (2 Cor. 12:9 NLT).

Today, when worry creeps into my thoughts, I recognize it for what it is—a red flag warning. And with biblical truth to temper my own emotions, I offer the prayer strategies in this book as offensive weapons for your battle to attain peace and rest.

The most effective strategy I can offer when faced with any crisis is to seek God first. Sometimes mere words and prayers spoken by others fail to penetrate our thoughts and feelings. But God's Word promises to help us when we're weak:

> [T]he Spirit helps us in our weakness. We do not
> know what we ought to pray for, but the Spirit himself
> intercedes for us through wordless groans. And he
> who searches our hearts knows the mind of the Spirit,
> because the Spirit intercedes for God's people in accordance with the will of God. (Rom. 8:26–27 NIV)

I offer you this short prayer that emerged during a lengthy family crisis when I was incapable of knowing what to ask God to do for us:

> *Father, I need you, but I don't know what to say.*
> *Thank you for your Spirit, who guides me when I pray.*
> *Spirit, intercede—you alone know my needs.*[2]

Part One

Red Flags

Raising Up a Standard of Truth

When the enemy shall come in like a flood,

the Spirit of the Lord shall lift up a standard against him.

(Isa. 59:19 KJV)

Warnings

....

*Navigating Your Negative Self-Talk
and Overwhelming Anxiety*

*Raise a signal flag as a warning for Jerusalem:
"Flee now! Do not delay!" (Jer. 4:6 NLT)*

I've struggled with restlessness most my life. Just ask my family. My Aunt Jo politely informed me that I was always a "bit stubborn," regularly testing the boundaries set for me as a child.

I don't recall much about my childhood, but those who knew me best then seem to agree with Aunt Jo's assessment. My routine battles with worry even now, later in life, also confirm her opinion.

My mother, a strong-willed perfectionist, knew how to rein me into submission. My resistance became obvious at an early age as she applied her special regimen of discipline to her oldest daughter.

I recall one of my earliest memories of Mother's control tactics—resisting her daily ritual of brushing my hair.

"Karen Elizabeth, hold still!"

I learned to pay close attention to Mother's demands when she employed my middle name. Her shouts made me hold my breath as I prepared for unkind words. Her anger provoked all kinds of negative emotions within me—fear, anger, worry, and shame—that even today can be triggered by a bad hair moment.

Often Mother enforced her authority over me as she pulled my long, brown, curly hair into a ponytail. My neck snapped as she jerked my head back. I squirmed on the ladder-back kitchen chair as she pressed the hard-bristle brush into my scalp like a plow turning unbroken soil.

My brow furrowed, but Mother ignored my frown as she wrapped a tight rubber band around my ponytail. I learned to hold back the tears because resisting would only invite more harsh words.

If I flinched, Mother would pull my hair tighter and remind me of her authority using her curt sarcasm, "You know what's under a pony's tail, Miss Priss?"

I doubt that I ever met Mother's standard of the ideal, well-behaved child she hoped to show off in our small Texas community, but her strong-arm tactics proved to be an effective strategy to clean up her little tomboy before school each morning.

I enjoyed competing with my older brother and cousins—climbing trees, riding bikes, and playing ball. Most of the girls in my neighborhood played indoors with dolls, including my younger sister Cathy and my cousin, Marilyn, who wore leg braces after surviving childhood polio. I preferred the outdoors; I certainly did not intend to waste much time in Mother's kitchen, staying under her thumb.

Aunt Jo, Marilyn's mom, recalls that she only saw me cry once or twice as a child. But Mother didn't allow whining and complaining. So I learned to suppress my feelings and to brush my own hair at a very young age—without Mother's help.

I still resist authority figures at times, but I've discovered some helpful ways to control my emotions when threatened by someone's intrusion into my personal space.

My stubborn, restless spirit still challenges me, but I believe it is a strength that God gave me. It helps me maintain my sanity during difficult and confusing times as I persevere, pursuing dreams that I would have otherwise given up on long ago—like writing books.

My anxiety also nudges me to seek spiritual answers to define and understand the potholes and roadblocks in my path. And my childhood experiences proved the importance of recognizing the red flag warnings at each stage of my life.

Now I understand my frustration as a child resisting my mother's instructions. And I can relate to others who also struggle under their God-chosen authorities.

I laughed with Mother about her ponytail pressure later in life—even during her last days. She knew I forgave her parenting mistakes. As a child, I didn't recognize the stresses in her life or appreciate the fact that she was providing for a family with four children with a limited income in the Bible Belt.

I became less judgmental of her when I repeated her critical words in my own parenting mishaps. I still watch for those emotional warning signs when I visit my children and grandchildren.

I'm not alone in my struggle with my emotions—many women suffer with symptoms of anxiety and stress that impact their relationships, along with their mental, physical, emotional, and spiritual health.

I've discovered the Bible offers powerful strategies to help us overcome our anxious thoughts so we can experience the rest and peace that we need. And in my faith journey, I've noticed that many women also endure crises in their spiritual walk, spurring their God-given emotions of fear, doubt, and unbelief.

A Lesson from Parenting

When I was a child, I spoke and thought and reasoned as a child.
But when I grew up, I put away childish things. (1 Cor. 13:11 NLT)

My daughter, Tara, taught me the concept of identifying *red flags*—emotional warning signs—when we discussed the sibling rivalry between two of her five children.

Yes, I said *five* children. I had a tough time with just two! And I'm keenly aware of my shortcomings after forty years of marriage, with two married children and seven grandkids.

Tara still amazes me. She overcame difficult physical limitations as a child and continues to outperform my expectations, particularly in her parenting and teaching skills. After courageously facing and rising above judgment and shame as a teenage mom, she graduated with high honors from college with degrees in early childhood, gifted, and special education. Now, as a stay-at-home mom, Tara employs her training, talents, and skills to nurture her own children and encourage other parents.

As Tara's boys began to argue and struggle with their escalating outbursts of anger, she realized that their behavior was an indication of a deeper heart issue that couldn't be fixed with negative consequences alone. But she was prepared for the challenge. She taught her children to understand and recognize their own emotional warning signs, helping them develop self-control and find alternative ways to solve their problems.

Tara encourages her children to not be ashamed of their God-given emotions. Genesis 1:26 says that God created human beings in his image to reflect his nature.

Ecclesiastes 3:1–8 reminds us, "There is a time for everything . . . a time to weep and a time to laugh, a time to mourn and a time to dance" (NIV).

God created our emotions, and he warns us when a problem surfaces so we can control our reactions. Responding to our natural emotions can challenge us all.

Tara used a smoke detector analogy to help her children relate to their emotional responses. She reminded them how they often overreact with their initial emotions, "When you hear the smoke alarm beep, you don't always scream 'Fire!' and stop, drop, and roll out of the house."

To teach them more about their natural responses, Tara explained, "You also don't pull the smoke detector off the wall and rip out the batteries."

Tara wanted to help her children understand the reason for their emotional outbursts so they could learn to stop and figure out why they are feeling angry before they responded impulsively. She warned them, "Don't freak out—find the source of whatever triggered the alarm."

Some emotions could be compared to a 911 emergency call—like witnessing abusive behavior. But we all need to respond appropriately to our personal alarm triggers.

For instance, some emotional warnings could be compared to an alarm for a small fire. These can't be ignored—if left alone, they can become dangerous. But you may be able to extinguish those fires yourself or get help to repair the damage in the near future.

I think even parents might tend to overreact with this kind of emotional red flag—like losing your temper after finding evidence of a child's exposure to or experimenting with pornography, drugs, or alcohol.

When we first sense anger, like when we initially hear the smoke alarm, it's important to investigate quickly without panicking. Burnt toast can cause the detector to beep in the same way a personality conflict can quickly trigger anger. Both problems need to be addressed, but neither is a reason to panic. It's important to recognize that we can be easily offended or tempted to overreact because of our feelings, just like a smoke detector can malfunction or detect the scent of a harmless candle.

I applaud how this teaching can help us all discover the actual source of our emotional triggers so we can diagnose our problems and respond appropriately.

Tara says, "I teach my kids to pray first, even if it's just a quick 'Help me, God.'"

Reality Check

Don't shrink. Don't puff up. Just stand your sacred ground.
(Brené Brown)[3]

How can I write a book about worry while I'm still one of the most anxious people I know?

I revisited my question as I decided to approach this topic. *Can I claim to be an authority on the subject of anxiety?* Perhaps. I've wrestled with perfectionism for years. Plus, I've sensed the Lord leading me to tell the stories that matter most to me. And he's exposed me to difficult lessons about worry in the waiting rooms of my life.

Yet I'm reluctant to confess that I questioned my ability to write about both my experiences and anxiety in general—just ask those who know me best. Long before this was published, one of my friends joked, "How's that book you're *not* writing coming along?"

As I attempted to write and handle my other obligations, there were many times when I experienced panic attacks, headaches, and other annoying, worrisome distractions. For me, trying to juggle too many commitments at once can provoke emotional outbursts, which ultimately stem from negative thoughts and my tendency to become overwhelmed by worry. To be honest, multitasking falls into the same category as many other important things in life for me—impossible!

I just don't seem to finish some important projects. Can you relate?

Every time I start a new exercise program or just take a walk around the block, something seems to get in the way, like bad weather, an illness, an injury, or just fatigue.

Discouraging thoughts overwhelm me, and I am left wondering if I will ever be able to discipline myself enough to lose these extra pounds—evidence of my emotional eating habits. The older I get, the harder it becomes to break habits. And when I focus on what I should not eat, I'm tempted even more to eat what is not healthy.

> I can anticipate the response that is coming: "I know that all God's commands are spiritual, but I'm not. Isn't this also your experience?" Yes. I'm full of myself—after all, I've spent a long time in sin's prison. What I don't understand about myself is that I decide one way, but then I act another, doing things I absolutely despise. So if I can't be trusted to figure out what is best for myself and then do it, it becomes obvious that God's command is necessary. (Rom. 7:14–16 *The Message*)

How can we readily recognize the warning signs of worry? For me, I finally admitted that I couldn't figure out the answer myself. Once I did this, it became obvious that I needed to seek help beyond my own logic. For me, the Bible offered the guidance and wisdom I needed.

You may struggle with similar issues. In fact, this may be the reason you picked up this book—hoping for a catalyst to move you to solutions and to release you from daily worries.

Why can't I defeat my negative thinking by my own willpower? The Bible identifies the source of our temptation to give in to worry:

> For we are not fighting against flesh-and-blood enemies,
> but against evil rulers and authorities of the unseen
> world, against mighty powers in this dark world, and
> against evil spirits in the heavenly places. (Eph. 6:12 NLT)

I found that truth empowered me to resist attacks from a supernatural enemy. But even as I tried to invoke scriptural truth for my life, another crisis would surface. Or I would entertain another random worrisome thought. *Why can't I keep up with my daily commitments? Why can't I just do what I need to do?*

Each time I stray from focusing on God's truth, I ask him for help, and he points me to the promises in his Word to guide me:

> No test or temptation that comes your way is beyond
> the course of what others have had to face. All you need
> to remember is that God will never let you down; he'll
> never let you be pushed past your limit; he'll always
> be there to help you come through it. (1 Cor. 10:13
> *The Message*)

When I worried about finishing this book, I counted on this promise in Philippians:

> And I am certain that God, who began the good work
> within [me], will continue his work until it is finally
> finished on the day when Christ Jesus returns. (Phil.
> 1:6 NLT)

Has God fulfilled that promise to me? Well—here you are reading this book, right?

Observing Worry's Red Flags

Why are you down in the dumps, dear soul? Why are you crying the blues? Fix my eyes on God—soon I'll be praising again. He puts a smile on my face. He's my God. (Ps. 42:11 The Message)

Circumstances can force us to feel out of control when negative thoughts trigger harmful emotions, like worry, anger, or fear. And these red flag warnings compound other pressing problems to threaten our physical and spiritual health.

A few years ago, my husband Dan and I traveled to our hometown, where we visited old friends. On our return trip, I shared a concern with Dan. Some of my friends were afflicted by anxiety-related symptoms, taking mood-altering medications to calm their nerves and suffering in silence. *And I thought I was the only one!*

Most of my friends professed faith in Christ. Yet here they were suffering from symptoms of anxiety. Although I do think medication is appropriate at times, I also believe we *all* need spiritual help. No one can endure a crisis without experiencing anxiety unless she is prepared in advance for the challenges.

When I examined the definition of *emotions*, it confirmed my belief that God gave me emotions for a good purpose. According to the Oxford dictionary, an emotion is a "natural instinctive state of mind deriving from one's circumstances, mood, or relationships with others."

I know many women who suffer from anxiety, migraines, insomnia, and nightmares. A few are held hostage by their emotions, avoiding contact with other people, while neglecting important responsibilities at home and work. Many evidence low self-esteem and stay tense or angry most of their days.

I heard my friends' confessions, privately admitting to crying from sadness, frustration, and depression. As they acknowledged their pain, they also indicated that their dependence on stress medication was a source of shame or humiliation. I may be treading on your toes as I mention my friends' depending on medication. But I'm also admitting my own struggles. Other signs of stress include hyperfocus, confusion, bad decisions, forgetfulness, perfectionism, self-criticism, and self-deprecation.

Some of my friends and family will laugh as they read this because they know I display these characteristics at times. And I sadly admit that my frustrations only make my life harder—especially when writing a book about worry.

Our worrying and unbridled anxiety may bring irreparable damage to our most important relationships. Our lashing out might provoke unexpected consequences. Or we may become people pleasers. We may try to control everything around us. Anxious thoughts fuel our restlessness, hopelessness, unbelief, fear, disobedience, and doubt.

Do you find yourself avoiding others? Worry, stress, and anxiety could well be the root cause of your despair and isolation.

Do you share the feelings of this scripture? "I do not understand what I do. For what I want to do I do not do, but what I hate I do" (Rom. 7:15 NIV).

For these reasons and many more, I share my battle with worry. No, I haven't found a final solution to my problems. Red flags still fly high during difficult circumstances. But I now have an effective strategy that helps me navigate negative thoughts and dodge the panic attacks that threaten my effectiveness.

Now I hope to choose to seek God at the slightest hint of worry—this red flag lets me know I'm moving toward full-blown panic if I don't bridle my thoughts. I now know the purpose of the emotional warnings in my life—they call attention to my weaknesses and expose my ongoing need for God to live in peace in my world.

What do I say to myself when I see the red flags of worry waving high? I speak God's truth to my own soul—or as I prefer to call it, *GraceTalk*.

In the next chapter, I'll unpack a little of what I've concluded about this GraceTalk.

GraceTalk

Speaking God's Truth to Your Soul

God means what he says. What he says goes. His powerful Word is sharp as a surgeon's scalpel, cutting through everything, whether doubt or defense, laying us open to listen and obey. Nothing and no one is impervious to God's Word. We can't get away from it—no matter what. (Heb. 4:12 The Message)

"You know what killed that squirrel?" my husband mused as we drove through our Arkansas neighborhood.

Duh, I thought. *A car ran over him.*

"Indecision," he explained.

Dan always seems to think in black or white terms—no gray areas. "If you don't like carrots, don't eat them. If you hate working as a secretary, find another job."

"Indecision?" I asked suspiciously. "Wait a minute. Are you comparing me to that squirrel?"

Dan and I are living proof that opposites attract in relationships, especially in marriage. But after over forty years of marriage, I think I'm finally embracing a few decisive traits from my husband—like how to organize my office and how to plan and follow through on my dreams.

For example, every year I adopt several New Year's resolutions. But by springtime, I'm darting back and forth, like an insecure squirrel crossing the road. My mind bounces between doubts and fears. *Is this plan even possible? What about my failure to follow through on all those other projects? Will this just be another waste of my time and resources?*

As I tried to dismiss my anxious thoughts, this question from Matthew 6:27 caught my attention: "Can any one of you by worrying add a single hour to your life?" (NIV).

Could my worry and indecision close the doors to many of my dreams and plans? God's Word continued to speak truth to my soul.

Jeremiah 29:11–12 promises, "For I know the plans I have for you . . . plans to prosper you and not to harm you, plans to give you hope and a future. Then you will call on me and come and pray to me, and I will listen to you" (NIV).

Can I discover God's plans for my life as I seek him in prayer? Could it be that simple?

In Jeremiah 29:13–14, we find another promise: "You will seek me and find me when you seek me with all your heart. I will be found by you" (NIV).

So what have I resolved about my indecision and worry? Now I know the importance of speaking God's truth into my life—or as I prefer to call it, GraceTalk.

God's recorded promises help me stay focused on his truth instead of entertaining negative thoughts, which rob me of my peace and rest. As I choose to focus all my thoughts on God's promises, I also try to count my blessings instead of listing my problems.

If you don't know what you're doing, pray to the Father. He loves to help. You'll get his help, and won't be condescended to when you ask for it. Ask boldly, believingly, without a second thought. People who "worry their prayers" are like wind-whipped waves. Don't think you're going to get anything from the Master that way, adrift at sea, keeping all your options open. (James 1:5–8 *The Message*)

Embracing GraceTalk

Are you tired? Worn out? Burned out on religion? Come to me. Get away with me and you'll recover your life. I'll show you how to take a real rest . . . Learn the unforced rhythms of grace. (Matt. 11:28–29 The Message*)*

In response to my anxiety and worry, I consulted the Bible for answers to my restless nature and lack of focus. And I found myself in good company. Most of the people in the Bible lost hope at some point during their journeys. They also sought God for direction and answers in their difficult circumstances. But God did not always remove their problems. He often gave them his promises instead, to enable them to face their challenges.

In 2 Corinthians 12, the apostle Paul boasts of his sufferings and weaknesses:

Because of the extravagance of those revelations, and so I wouldn't get a big head, I was given the gift of a handicap to keep me in constant touch with my limitations. Satan's angel did his best to get me down; what he in fact did was push me to my knees. No danger then of walking around high and mighty! At first I didn't think of it as a gift, and begged God to remove it. Three times I did that, and then he told me,

> *My grace is enough; it's all you need.*
> *My strength comes into its own in your weakness.*
> Once I heard that, I was glad to let it happen. I
> quit focusing on the handicap and began appreciating
> the gift. It was a case of Christ's strength moving in
> on my weakness. Now I take limitations in stride, and
> with good cheer, these limitations that cut me down to
> size—abuse, accidents, opposition, bad breaks. I just let
> Christ take over! And so the weaker I get, the stronger I
> become. (2 Cor. 12:7–10 *The Message*)

Under pressure, I still don't think of my weaknesses as "gifts."
Should something that restricts my ability to function physically,
mentally, or socially be considered a "gift"?

A "thorn in the flesh" seems a bit closer to describing my weaknesses, since they are irritating, causing physical pain, mental confusion, emotional trauma, and ongoing problems. In fact, I won't
record the phrase I'm thinking of right now—it's not suitable for
this genre. But speaking of inappropriate words—that describes
another weakness that I've battled most of my life.

When I'm frustrated and tired, ungodly and demeaning
words sometimes roll off my anxious tongue. I've asked the Lord
to remove that tendency. And I'm always reminded of his promise
of grace each time I'm tempted to respond in anger.

My failures continue to sting. But did you notice God's response
to Paul's plea for relief? "My grace is all you need. My power works
best in weakness" (2 Cor. 12:9 NLT).

I do not relish admitting my weaknesses and being reminded
of my failures. Honestly, my confession takes me beyond my comfort zone, and I know others who share this same struggle. Yet I
am aware that your problems may be more difficult than simply
following through on a writing project, exercising, eating healthier,
or responding with uncontrolled expletives before thinking.

Maybe you've asked God to help you as you try to manage an abusive relationship. Perhaps you're asking Him to help you stop verbally lashing out at someone—maybe your own children. Or you may feel helpless about your mental or physical disabilities. Have you begged God to take away your problems of addiction or depression?

You may be discouraged right now because of a tragedy in your family. I've even shaken my fist at God, taking my frustrations out on him when a tragedy swept over my family.

Have you been the target of hypercritical Christians in your church or family? Are you determined to be different? I've been in church all my life. I've witnessed critical spirits and judgmental attitudes. At times, they even have shown up in my own mirror.

Yes, I still wrestle with worry, and I have been "burned out on religion" more than once. But I have learned the importance of speaking God's truth to my soul—GraceTalk. I encourage you to consider it the next time you sense emotional red flags waving in your own life.

Applying GraceTalk to Worry

*We're going to have to let truth scream louder to our souls
than the lies that have infected us. (Beth Moore)[4]*

I first recognized the power of GraceTalk as I dealt with intense grief following my dad's death. As I faced the first Christmas season without my dad, I couldn't avoid the sadness and grief, especially since he died on December 26th. My mother had remarried, and my family was in disarray, trying to deal with all the changes in our lives.

For years, a cloud of sadness hung over Christmas as I silently grieved over the absence of my dad. I worried about my own future. My grandmother died of pancreatic cancer; then my dad succumbed to the same disease. *Was I next?*

When I experienced a strange health symptom, I remembered Dad's pain. Predictably, I feared the worst. As I attempted to address my melancholy thoughts, I found peace of mind by refocusing on a promise from the Bible instead of my painful loss.

Several years after Dad's death, I discovered this powerful scripture that helped me reconcile my fears and my questions about his untimely demise at the age of forty-seven:

> Good people pass away; the godly often die before their time. But no one seems to care or wonder why. No one seems to understand that God is protecting them from the evil to come. For those who follow godly paths will rest in peace when they die. (Isa. 57:1–2 NLT)

I recited the passage over and over again. *What does this scripture mean? How does that apply to Dad's death? Did God guide me to this scripture for a particular purpose?*

I read it again, wanting the words to be fixed in my mind so I would never forget them. It helped me comprehend that Dad's death spared him from more pain. And this powerful Word brought peace to my heart and my mind as I repeated God's truth to my grief-filled soul.

I imagined my dad in heaven, where "God himself will be with [him]. He will wipe every tear from [his] eyes, and there will be no more death or sorrow or crying or pain. All these things are gone forever" (Rev. 21:3–4 NLT).

At the time of my loss, I would have preferred that my dad be healed so that I could have him by my side as I journeyed through my own adulthood. Now I believe that my heavenly Father redeemed that loss for me, using it as a catalyst to drive me to seek him with my concerns.

I shared the verse with my brother and sisters. I read it to my husband. I quoted it to others who grieved. I wanted them to experience the peace God provided with these words. But at that time, I did not comprehend just how powerful God's Word can be in our lives.

How did my anxiety about my Dad's death lead me to reconcile the pain and the emptiness inside my heart? This epiphany sparked a relentless search for more truth in God's Word. And I would never be the same.

God speaks to all our problems in the Bible, but we must ask for his guidance. James 4:2 says, "[Y]ou don't have what you want because you don't ask God for it" (NLT).

So I searched for answers about worry in God's Word. And I found that Jesus encouraged us to not to fret over our problems.

In Matthew 6, Jesus said these things about worry:

> But seek first his kingdom and his righteousness, and
> all these things will be given to you as well. Therefore
> do not worry about tomorrow, for tomorrow will worry
> about itself. Each day has enough trouble of its own.
> (Matt. 6:33–34 NIV)

How did I begin to seek his kingdom and his righteousness in my life? First, I began on my knees—praying, seeking God for help, and asking him to reveal his promises and to empower me to believe his Word.

One morning, I woke up early to pray. But instead of praying, I could not take my focus away from a family problem. Before long, I had created a long list of fears that fed my negative, anxious thoughts and doubts about the future.

Then the realization of my incessant worrying made me place my worries on hold as I prayed, *Lord, how do I stop worrying?*

As soon as I voiced my prayer, I recalled another familiar passage in the Bible:

> I know what it is to be in need, and I know what it is to
> have plenty. I have learned the secret of being content

> in any and every situation, whether well fed or hungry,
> whether living in plenty or in want. I can do all this
> through him who gives me strength. (Phil. 4:12–13 NIV)

I chose to exchange my anxious thoughts for promises from God's Word. And I asked him to give me the strength I needed and to teach me the secret of contentment. Then the blessings of that promise emerged, replacing my list of problems. I stopped, dropped, and prayed again, offering him a prayer of thanks.

As important as the Bible is to our Christian faith, I believe there are many Christian women who do not know how to apply biblical principles to their daily problems and concerns. We may be aware the Bible warns us not to be anxious about anything, but we might not know how to stop worrying. I didn't. We may mask our worries for a time, but in the heat of a crisis, we willingly shed our disguises.

You may be confined to a waiting room right now, dealing with a threatening situation or about to make a life-changing decision. Worry may feel like a dark storm cloud. And you feel the suffocating grip of your anxiety. Fear and panic set in. You can't breathe. You feel trapped. You look for an escape, but there is none. Where can we find hope for such times?

> For though we live in the world, we do not wage war as
> the world does. The weapons we fight with are not the
> weapons of the world. On the contrary, they have divine
> power to demolish strongholds. We demolish argu-
> ments and every pretension that sets itself up against the
> knowledge of God, and we take captive every thought to
> make it obedient to Christ. (2 Cor. 10:3–5 NIV)

If we are going to be able to take every thought captive successfully, we must learn to speak God's truth—GraceTalk—to our unbridled and often destructive emotions so we can navigate through the murky waters of worry and anxiety.

Sharing My Stories

"I've tried to stop worrying, but I just can't seem to quit."

As I listened to Kathy share problems about her family, I wanted to respond with what I knew about worry. *Can I help my friend? How can I offer spiritual truths so deeply rooted in my own personal experiences?*

I identified with some of Kathy's issues. But I could only share my point of view as a follower of Christ, not a counselor or expert; I can only claim professional credentials as a writer and writing instructor. But I also know that many times, healing comes through telling our stories to others.

Then I thought of all we have in common. Kathy and I met at church over four decades ago, so our friendship has always been based on our faith and our family connections.

When Kathy's family moved to a nearby community, we continued to visit until my family moved to attend seminary—about three hundred miles away. Kathy and I lost touch for many years as I adapted to my new life away from my family and friends. I longed to find another good friend like Kathy.

When I thought to contact Kathy, I had been in my hometown with my mother-in-law following the death of Dan's father. We met at a local restaurant for breakfast one morning. So much had happened in our lives, it became impossible to catch up in one short hour. We exchanged contact information and promised to stay in touch in the coming days.

Kathy and I reconnected when she and her husband vacationed in Arkansas. We shared several meals together. Our conversation explored our personal lives, as they had in the past. I'm amazed how some relationships just resume and go forward, even after decades of silence.

Our conversations naturally went back to our families. I shared my struggle with writing about worry. And she shared her desire to let go of her nagging concerns. We discussed our growth in faith over the past thirty years.

As I told Kathy about my experiences with anxiety, I realized that she represented many women I know who struggle with worry. I found it very challenging to share the truths I had gained from my waiting room experiences with her during our short visit, even though I write about these truths daily, speak to groups of women about them, and discuss them with friends and family often.

So what are the basic tenets gleaned from my experiences? And how do I plan to present them to you within the context of this book?

The previous chapter discusses what my daughter and I define as red flags of worry. Looking ahead, I will describe my crisis of faith and the beginning of my personal relationship with Christ.

From there, I'll walk you down a short journey through some of the basic spiritual truths I learned from difficult seasons of my life. God's Word undergirds the foundation of my faith. And I hold on tightly during the whirlwinds of my life.

I know that everyone's experiences are as varied as the storms that roll in and out of our lives. But I also know that God is the Creator of the universe. He can speak his Word to our hearts during the crises of our lives, offering peace and rest.

Even though the red flags of worry can flap violently in turbulent wind, I have learned to treat such warning signs as a reminder to stop, drop, and pray as I choose to seek God for direction, peace, and refuge from the onslaught of life-changing events.

GraceTalk—speaking God's truth to my soul—continues to help me overcome my troubling thoughts. And I still must remind myself of the promise of REST from Philippians 4:5–9, as I choose to remember, exalt, surrender, and trust.

How do I search for God? Follow me through some powerful lessons I've learned about seeking God when our burdens are heavy and hard to endure. I'll examine some important aspects of my own faith walk, including solitude, silence, prayer, listening, and waiting.

What if you've never considered seeking God before? Do you still have doubts about God's existence?

I am convinced God desires a relationship with us all. I'll share a story later about the times that God pursued me, even when I wasn't aware of him. The Bible promises that he will seek out his lost sheep:

> Suppose one of you had a hundred sheep and lost one. Wouldn't you leave the ninety-nine in the wilderness and go after the lost one until you found it? When found, you can be sure you would put it across your shoulders, rejoicing, and when you got home call in your friends and neighbors, saying, "Celebrate with me! I've found my lost sheep!" Count on it—there's more joy in heaven over one sinner's rescued life than over ninety-nine good people in no need of rescue. (Luke 15:4–7 *The Message*)

These words may be evidence that God is seeking you right now. So I pray you'll stop and consider that miraculous possibility.

The truths I present are based on personal experiences and my understanding of God's messages provided in the Bible. Some of my stories may also raise a red flag of doubt for you. So I pray you will take those warnings as signals to you to seek God for yourself.

Your faith in God cannot be based on my experiences or anyone else's. But the Word of God has proven to be trustworthy as a guide for our lives—an avenue for reconciliation with him and others the Lord leads our way. God wants an intimate relationship with you. He knows your needs. And he knows the reasons you're hurting.

Do I still have crises of faith? Absolutely. And I believe I'm not the only one. So in the next chapter, I'll share the story of an early struggle of my own. We'll also examine a chapter from Moses's life where he struggled with his faith in God and with himself.

3

Crisis of Faith

∙∙∙

Facing Your Fear, Doubt, and Unbelief

Now my soul is troubled, and what shall I say?
"Father, save me from this hour"?
No, it was for this very reason I came to this hour. (John 12:27 NIV)

My life changed when I faced the challenge of writing my faith story for the first time.

During our application process to enroll in the seminary, my husband Dan and I were required to provide a written life history that centered on our faith. Even though I had been a lifelong church member, I struggled with that assignment. As I tried to remember the details surrounding my conversion and baptism, I could not recall much, which initiated a spiritual crisis for me.

I pictured myself as a scrawny, nine-year-old tomboy with a long, brown, curly ponytail proudly dressed in my Blue Bird uniform. Blue Birds, part of the Camp Fire Girls organization, offered girls ages nine through ten "exploration of ideas and creative play built around family and community life."[5]

I sat next to my friend Bibbie in the sanctuary of our hometown church—our mothers had lined us all up in the second pew for Camp Fire Girls recognition day.

Bibbie and I had talked about "joining the church" after watching other kids our age being baptized by our pastor.

"Wanna get baptized?" Bibbie asked.

I shrugged my shoulders, nodded, and agreed without a moment's hesitation, "OK!"

So we slid out of our pew, walked down the church aisle to our pastor, and told him that we wanted to get baptized. I can imagine what we looked like as we walked down the aisle.

My baptism experience seemed unremarkable, similar to those of most people I knew back then—except for my husband Dan. Tears came to my eyes when I read Dan's testimony of faith included with his seminary application. I had observed an unexpected change in him after he decided to follow Christ. He seemed to know Jesus in a personal way, and he even talked openly about his faith and studied his Bible every day. At that time, I considered my faith a very private matter.

What did it really mean to follow Christ? I tried to talk to God in prayer, but I didn't know what to say. After we moved to the seminary campus, I continued seeking answers by studying my Bible and reading books written by Christian authors.

One book in particular caught my attention since the author, Jack Taylor, was a member of our new church. In *The Key to Triumphant Living*, Jack shared his personal testimony of discovering the mystery of the gospel, "which is Christ in you, the hope of glory" (Col. 1:27 NIV).[6]

The words "Christ in you" stirred my heart. Trying to understand the meaning of that phrase, I turned to Galatians 2:20: "My old self has been crucified with Christ. It is no longer I who live, but Christ lives in me" (NLT).

I read the passage aloud, trying to internalize its meaning. But when I thought of Christ, I visualized him in heaven with God, the all-powerful Creator of the universe. I had even sensed God's peace at the time of my dad's death, but I'd never sensed Christ living inside me.

I was overwhelmed with depression about my marriage, motherhood, my children's health issues, and my mother's untimely remarriage following my dad's death. My vulnerable emotions choked the life out of me.

I had admired my dad's quiet confidence and faith, even as cancer ravaged his body. He never complained, even when some overtly judged his lack of faith to be healed. Although one particular visitor's comments were delivered with a gentle pat and a smile at his hospital bedside, her words were laced with criticism and judgment.

I bit my lip to rein in the impulse to return the offense.

But Dad just smiled and affirmed his trust in God to heal him, even if he had to wait until heaven.

Dad did not fear death. I heard him talking to Jesus from his hospital bed following one of his surgeries. At first, I thought an old friend had stopped by to see him, so I peeked in, not wanting to disturb them. Dad was alone, but I knew he had been in touch with heaven.

During Dad's last agonizing hours, I sensed a peace all around him. And in the stillness of those moments, sunrays beamed down through the hospital window, illuminating his room. With his last breath, his countenance changed—from gripping agony to a peaceful rest.

Although I experienced a measure of God's peace then, I still wondered if the Spirit of Christ lived inside of every believer, even though I never doubted that his Spirit lived inside my dad.

Why was I so unsure about my own faith? *What does it really mean to be a follower of Christ?* But my own doubts and fears consumed my thoughts.

All my life, I had tried to do things that I had been taught to please God. I never skipped a church service or event. I scheduled a devotional time every day. I attempted to control my anger toward my kids and my husband. But it never seemed enough. The bad decisions from my past constantly haunted me, reminding me of my great need for reconciliation with God.

Did believing in Jesus require that I know him in a personal way? Was that possible? I believed in him just like I believed the facts about other historical heroes. But I had never met them face to face. Was it enough to just believe he had lived and died to pay for the sins of humanity? *Did he really die for my sake?*

On my quest for truth, one verse helped me discover that true faith in Jesus requires more than simply believing in his existence: "You believe that there is one God. Good! Even the demons believe that—and shudder" (James 2:19 NIV).

When Jesus's disciples asked him to show them the way to heaven, "Jesus answered, 'I am the way and the truth and the life. No one comes to the Father except through me'" (John 14:6 NIV).

I did not doubt that Jesus had been executed and died on a cross so I could be forgiven. But I realized that I had never really asked him to forgive *me* for *my* sins.

I thought of a picture I had seen at church as a child, depicting Jesus knocking on a door. And I realized he had been knocking on the door of my heart for a long time, but I had never invited him in.

I'm not sure of the exact words I prayed—probably, "Jesus, help! I need you!"

Then, I simply confessed my faith to the Lord in prayer and asked for his forgiveness. I needed his presence and his peace within me.

No lightning bolts. No thunder claps. But from that moment on, I sensed his ever-present peace within me. Now I know the Lord is always with me, especially now, as I pen these words.

The fear of embarrassment and humiliation kept me from responding to the Holy Spirit's promptings in my teens. But after I accepted Christ, I still hesitated from telling anyone.

Eventually, I confronted my fears as I shared my newfound faith with my mother, but she questioned my decision. So we spent many hours in long-distance conversations, discussing our beliefs and my decision. I knew it might take a miracle, but I continued to pray that somehow the Lord would reconcile our personal differences and our spiritual convictions.

> Dear friends, do not be surprised at the fiery ordeal
> that has come on you to test you, as though something
> strange were happening to you. (1 Pet. 4:12 NIV)

Red Flags of Faith

Moses said to God, "Why are you treating me this way? What did I ever do to you to deserve this? . . . I can't do this by myself—it's too much . . . if this is how you intend to treat me, do me a favor and kill me. I've seen enough; I've had enough. Let me out of here." (Num. 11:14–15 The Message)

As I explored God's Word for relief from my anxiety, I found I was in good company. Even successful spiritual leaders struggled in their faith when challenged by unexpected changes or threatening events.

Consider Moses, who God chose to lead his people out of slavery. He avoided certain death in Egypt only to be relegated to tending herds in the desert for the next forty years. Then he encountered the impossibility of the task that God gave him—to lead his people to their promised land.

First Red Flag: Alarm

Moses was shepherding the flock of Jethro, his father-in-law, the priest of Midian. He led the flock to the west end of the wilderness and came to the mountain of God, Horeb. (Exod. 3:1 The Message)

There, alone on the mountain of God, Moses heard God's call to return to his homeland and lead his people to their promised land. As he tended his herds, he encountered a miraculous phenomenon—a supernatural burning bush. "The angel of God appeared to him in flames of fire blazing out of the middle of a bush. He looked. The bush was blazing away but it didn't burn up" (Exod. 3:2 *The Message*).

Try to imagine yourself all alone in the mountains, witnessing an unexpected blazing fire. But you don't run. Why? Because "the angel of God" appears in the flames and the bush is not consumed by the blaze. You're paralyzed by fear—you can't speak, think, or move. Then a voice from within the fire calls your name. *Could it be the voice of God?*

God's Promise

God warns Moses, "Don't come any closer. Remove your sandals from your feet. You're standing on holy ground" (Exod. 3:5 *The Message*).

I wonder how Moses felt. *Did his heart race? Could he breathe? Could he even speak? What do you say when the God of the universe speaks to you directly?*

God speaks again and reveals his identity: "I am the God of your father: The God of Abraham, the God of Isaac, the God of Jacob" (Exod. 3:6 *The Message*).

Moses covers his face, afraid to look upon the image of the holy God.

Then God's words resonate from the blazing bush as he issues instructions:

"The Israelite cry for help has come to me, and I've seen for myself how cruelly they're being treated by the Egyptians. It's time for you to go back: I'm sending you to Pharaoh to bring my people, the people of Israel, out of Egypt." (Exod. 3:9–10 *The Message*)

Personal Connection: Finding Peace

How does God speak to you? I woke up early one morning overwhelmed by my "to-do" list, so I decided to take a walk at sunrise. As I turned down the street toward the lake, the view of the sunrise greeted me. I dismissed all my worries and soaked in the beauty of the dawn.

I may not have experienced God speaking to me from a burning bush, but he has captured my attention with the majesty of glorious sunrises and sunsets. When he lights up the sky, I see evidence of his presence all around me.

Second Red Flag: Insecurity

Moses answered God, "But why me? What makes you think that I could ever go to Pharaoh and lead the children of Israel out of Egypt?" (Exod. 3:11 The Message)

Do what? Go where? Why me? I understand Moses's response, don't you? He knew that this assignment was well beyond his human ability—an impossible task. Aware of his weaknesses and the shallowness of his wisdom, Moses recounted his previous failures. He even questioned God's motives for asking him to accept such an assignment.

God's Reminder

Do you believe God was shocked by Moses's questions? I don't.

God responded to Moses's doubts with the promise of his presence instead of judgment: "I'll be with you . . . And this will be the proof that I am the one who sent you: When you have brought my people out of Egypt, you will worship God right here at this very mountain" (Exod. 3:12 *The Message*).

Personal Connection: Hearing God

I identify with Moses's insecurities. My doubts and questions don't surprise my all-knowing God either. I've learned not to trust my initial emotional responses when surprising events unfold.

As I prepared for my first college teaching assignment years ago as a graduate student, I experienced fear in a new way. *What if a student questions my authority? Who am I to be teaching college freshmen? I'm still a graduate student myself!*

Dan encouraged me, "Why are you doubting yourself, Karen? You've got the credentials to teach there."

After those affirming words, I was determined to conquer my natural fears. So I walked into the classroom prepared and confident in my ability and authority to do the job I was hired to do.

God provided solutions for my insecurities. I leaned on him for my confidence as I stepped forward to encourage college freshmen to improve their writing skills.

Third Red Flag: Fear of Judgment

Moses asked God, "Suppose I go to the People of Israel and I tell them, 'The God of your fathers sent me to you'; and they ask me, 'What is his name?' What do I tell them?" (Exod. 3:13 *The Message*).

What will people say? Moses voiced his insecurities and fear of judgment. How would he respond when people questioned his authority?

God's Reminder

Again, God answered Moses about his identity with a promise, "I-AM-WHO-I-AM. Tell the People of Israel, 'I-AM sent me to you'" (Exod. 3:14 *The Message*).

God told Moses exactly how to respond when his authority was doubted. He instructed Moses to tell the people he was the one who sent him. And God assured Moses he would be there, guiding every decision.

Personal Connection: Confronting Judgment

Has anyone ever challenged your authority? How did you respond? Have your fears ever tempted you to run away?

Jesus did not allow critics to hinder him from obeying God. In fact, when the religious leaders of his day tried to intimidate him, "Jesus responded by telling still more stories" (Matt. 22:1 *The Message*).

When I spoke of a faith experience to an intimate group of church friends, I was shocked by one of their responses. During my story, she rolled her eyes and started humming the theme to *The Twilight Zone*, a television series from the 1960s. I suddenly felt like an outsider, realizing my small group was no longer a safe place for me to share my faith.

I felt my blood pressure rise, and I resisted the urge to lash out with sharp, ungodly words. My heart raced. My head pounded. But I held my tongue as a scripture came to mind: "Don't use foul or abusive language. Let everything you say be good and helpful, so that your words will be an encouragement to those who hear them" (Eph. 4:29 NLT).

This person's rude comments provoked a typical response of anger within me. But God offered me an important lesson from this red flag experience. The Holy Spirit helped me control my words and avoid the conflict. Later, as the Lord addressed my wounded feelings, he prompted me to forgive her.

Since then, I've experienced similar criticism and judgment in a variety of situations, but I've chosen to continue telling my faith stories—as Jesus did when the legalists and unbelievers of his day mocked his words.

Fourth Red Flag: Fear of Rejection

Moses confessed another worrisome issue: "What if they do not believe me or listen to me and say, 'The Lord did not appear to you'?" (Exod. 4:1–2 NIV).

Moses feared others would not believe him and ignore him. He loathed the thoughts of their verbal attacks and the likelihood of being humiliated in the presence of many people.

God's Reminder

God offered two miraculous signs to illustrate and prove the promise of his supernatural presence and power. First, he called attention to Moses's staff: "What is that in your hand?" (Exod. 4:2 *The Message*).

As soon as Moses acknowledged the wooden staff in his hand and threw it down, it turned into a snake. Once again, imagine Moses's response. Frightened, he pulled back.

> Then the Lord said to him, "Reach out your hand and take it by the tail." So Moses reached out and took hold of the snake and it turned back into a staff in his hand. "This," said the Lord, "is so that they may believe that the Lord, the God of their fathers—the God of Abraham, the God of Isaac and the God of Jacob—has appeared to you." (Exod. 4:4–5 NIV)

God continued his object lessons with Moses, inflicting a dreaded disease on his hand, followed by complete restoration. Afterward, God gave Moses this promise:

> "If they do not believe you or pay attention to the first sign, they may believe the second. But if they do not believe these two signs or listen to you, take some water from the Nile and pour it on the dry ground. The

water you take from the river will become blood on the ground." (Exod. 4:8–9 NIV)

God knew doubters would confront Moses, so he promised to provide his supernatural presence and power to help him lead his people to their new land. And in the process, God transformed Moses, as he had done to his wooden staff.

Personal Connection: Facing Rejection

Can you sense how Moses felt? Have you ever felt God leading you to do something that you knew others would question or challenge?

Hoping for affirmation, I confided to a friend my desire to pursue writing, only to be challenged with, "What do *you* have to say?"

This heart-rending question wasn't meant to discourage me, but it echoed the doubt already troubling me: *What do I have to say? No one will believe me or listen to me! Why would anyone read anything I wrote?*

That question served as the motivation for me to seek God's guidance for specific direction: *What gifts and talents do I have? What skills do I need to develop? What resources are available to me?*

Could God transform the tools in your hand or use the resources available to you to fulfill his calling for your life? What do you have at hand that you could offer for the Lord's service? What resources has God already provided? A job or a career opportunity? Technology? The Internet? A skill, talent, or gift? Your training, education, or an academic opportunity? The people you know or see every day? Your church, family, and friends?

Fifth Red Flag: Timidity

Moses brought another objection: "Master, please, I don't talk well. I've never been good with words, neither before nor after you spoke to me. I stutter and stammer" (Exod. 4:10 *The Message*).

Moses acknowledged his inability to do what God asked him to do. He even elaborated about his weaknesses and inadequacies—his speaking, vocabulary, and a speech impediment. He claimed the task was impossible for him. But God had other plans.

When God spoke to Moses, he knew the impossibility of the task. But Moses's recognition of his human limitations proved to be one of his greatest leadership qualities—it forced him to acknowledge a dependence on God for everything.

God's Reminder

God responded to Moses with a series of rhetorical questions:

> "Who gave human beings their mouths? Who makes them deaf or mute? Who gives them sight or makes them blind? Is it not I, the Lord? Now go; I will help you speak and will teach you what to say." (Exod. 4:11–12 NIV)

Jesus made a similar commitment when he commissioned his disciples to spread the good news of his gospel:

> "Go out and train everyone you meet, far and near, in this way of life . . . instruct them in the practice of all I have commanded you. I'll be with you as you do this, day after day after day, right up to the end of the age." (Matt. 28:19–20 *The Message*)

Personal Connection: Embracing Truth

Each time I sense God directing me to abandon my comfort zone, my emotional red flags wave high. I'm often reminded of my limitations. I'm also tempted to focus on what other people will think of me.

I'm still not comfortable in exposing my weaknesses. And I confess—I still have moments of fear, doubt, and unbelief, just as Moses did.

I've heard many friends paralyzed by their own self-deprecating remarks as they express their inabilities to do what they need to do. These same excuses continue to cross my mind in my journey as a writer, teacher, blogger, and speaker. *Do I really have what it takes?*

What's the right answer? James 5:16 says,

> Confess your sins to each other and pray for each other so that you may be healed. The earnest prayer of a righteous person has great power and produces wonderful results. (NLT)

Red Flag Reflections

Do you have what it takes to do whatever God directs you to do? Have you defended your inaction with your own fears, doubts, and unbelief?

Whether you have had a life-changing faith experience or not, I'm sure you've encountered a few emotional red flag warnings designed to make you stop short of reaching your goals.

Moses experienced his burning bush sign in the wilderness—but God used the blistering blaze to captivate him. Then God called him to lead his people to their promised land. And as Moses responded with his fears, God guided him with his presence and power, fulfilling his promises to his people.

The red flag of worry distracted me the first time someone asked me to write down my faith story. I saw another flag waving as I faced my first teaching assignment in college. Then, as I pondered writing this book, my worries paralyzed me before I could follow the directions that God was providing. This chapter serves as a reminder to embrace our emotional flags, always expecting them to point us to the real truth revealed in God's promises.

I wish I had more confidence at times, like some folks I know. But I believe my awareness of limitations and weaknesses may be one of my strengths because it makes me dependent upon the

Lord's strength instead of my own. Today, more than ever, I am confident he will complete the work he has begun in me. And this is my prayer for you.

> I thank my God every time I remember you. In all my prayers for all of you, I always pray with joy because of your partnership in the gospel from the first day until now, being confident of this, that he who began a good work in you will carry it on to completion until the day of Christ Jesus. (Phil. 1:3–6 NIV)

Part Two

REST

Remember, Exalt, Surrender, and Trust

The Lord is near.

Do not be anxious about anything,

but in every situation, by prayer and petition,

with thanksgiving, present your requests to God.

And the peace of God, which transcends all understanding,

will guard your hearts and your minds in Christ Jesus.

(Phil. 4:5–7 NIV)

REST

Discovering a New Prayer Strategy

Don't fret or worry. Instead of worrying, pray. Let petitions and praises shape your worries into prayers, letting God know your concerns. Before you know it, a sense of God's wholeness, everything coming together for good, will come and settle you down. It's wonderful what happens when Christ displaces worry at the center of your life. (Phil. 4:6–7 The Message)

As Mother tried to rest in the hospital bed, I sat in a hard chair next to her with my laptop computer, editing a writing project. I felt trapped by my circumstances—unable to move toward my personal goals due to a family crisis.

I looked up, and Mother, who was watching me from her hospital bed, asked, "Is that your thesis?"

"Yes. I'm working on my revisions."

Mother continued to stare at me, so I stopped to talk to her, "Would you like for me to read it to you? It needs more work, and it always helps me to read aloud."

Mother perked up, "I'd love to hear it!"

"OK." I tried not to sound nervous.

Deep inside, I had a twinge of fear. The honest confessions revealed in my memoir could be painful for my mother. She didn't know about all my life experiences. But I took a deep breath and began reading it anyway, trusting God to cover my shame.

For the next two hours, I read while Mother listened. I cried, painfully unfolding my narrative, as Mother quietly took in my emotional response to my own words. About halfway through the manuscript, I paused and asked, "What do you think?" I needed a moment to regain my composure.

"I think people will be healed as they read it."

"You do?" Mother's honest words surprised and encouraged me, a welcomed breath of fresh air during the heaviness we felt from waiting on medical test results.

"In fact, I think I will be healed as you read it to me."

I nodded hopefully, wanting to appear strong for her. I didn't want to appear afraid in front of Mother. But I was grateful that she still had hope for good reports and her future.

I read to Mother most of the night until she questioned me about one of my stories.

"Who was your friend that died, Karen?"

"She was Dan's boss's wife." Shirley and her husband, Don, were our first friends in Arkansas.

After I explained my connection with Shirley, Mother tugged on the thin hospital blanket to cover her frail arms, asking to hear more about my friend.

We had prayed God might miraculously heal Shirley. But her health continued to decline, despite our prayers. When I went to visit her in the hospital, I became very discouraged as I observed her intense pain and suffering.

When I left, I simply prayed, "Lord, if healing is not the answer for Shirley here on earth, I pray you will give her your perfect healing and take her home to live with you forever in perfect health."

Shirley grew weaker each day in the hospital. And one morning, I awoke with a song from our church hymnal on my heart, "Softly and tenderly, Jesus is calling . . . come home, come home, ye who are weary come home."

In my spirit, I knew this message was for my friend. Shirley went home to be with Jesus that very day. I cried at her passing, yet I knew she was finally at peace.

When I finished reading the chapter about my friend, Mother said, "I liked the part about 'going home.'" Then she yawned as she adjusted her pillows.

"Are you tired, Mother?"

"Yes, but I hate to miss the ending."

"We'll finish reading it later, after you rest. Anyway, you know how this story ends." The memoir ended with the story of my first grandson's birth.

Without responding, Mother closed her eyes.

I put my revisions away and rearranged the chair to make it comfortable for the night.

As I relaxed, I pondered Mother's interest in Shirley's passing. I knew Mother feared for her own life. That was my primary reason for reading to her—to take her mind off of her own fears. And reading my thesis to her seemed to help her.

But as I remembered my promise to finish reading to her, I wondered, *Will I actually be able to fulfill that promise?*

Then I considered my comment to Mother about her knowing the end of my story, fearing that her life would be ending soon.

Before we left the hospital, Mother dealt with more than just her health issues. She talked about her worries and concerns again.

We also discussed forgiveness and prayed together. She asked the Lord to forgive her, and she thanked him for his grace toward her. She also asked him to help her forgive those who had caused her grief and pain.

Attending to Mother as she wrestled with such painful issues exhausted me. And I knew I needed to address my own problem with worry to find rest and peace. But I couldn't quit worrying about what to say to my mother as she faced the battle for her life.

Finding REST

The Lord is near. Do not be anxious about anything, but in every situation, by prayer and petition, with thanksgiving, present your requests to God. And the peace of God, which transcends all understanding, will guard your hearts and your minds in Christ Jesus.
(Phil. 4:5–7 NIV)

Can we find a remedy for worry?

When I first read verse six of Philippians 4, I thought, *Would it even be possible for me to not worry about* anything? *I've been anxious about almost* everything *for most of my adult life.*

As I continued to examine this particular scripture and pray about my own problem with anxiety, I developed a biblical strategy that helps me refocus my negative mind-set and meditate on God's promise of spiritual rest to overcome my ongoing battle with anxiety. Now when I'm tempted to worry, I know that I can choose to REST: remember, exalt, surrender, trust.

- *Remember*: "The Lord is near."
- *Exalt*: "[I]n every situation, by prayer and petition, with thanksgiving . . ."
- *Surrender*: ". . . present your requests to God."

- *Trust*: "And the peace of God, which transcends all understanding, will guard your hearts and your minds in Christ Jesus."

This REST acronym helps me fall asleep and find peace on many restless days. Dwelling on my regrets usually produces negative thoughts. But seeking God and meditating on the promises in his Word brings rest and peace to my heart and mind. Now when I focus on the pattern of REST, I can resist any attack of anxiety that comes my way.

How do I defeat anxiety with REST? First, I choose to focus on God's promises rather than my worries. Let me show you how it works for me.

One night, a wave of emotion rolled over me like a black cloud. Then an intense accusation unsettled my heart and my mind. Yet it sounded like my own voice: *How could I possibly write a book about REST? I am the most anxious person I know!*

Before I discovered REST, I would have pulled the covers over my head, fallen into deep depression, and believed the lies I heard. Thankfully, I've developed some strategic battle tactics, and I know how to face those attacks now.

So I stopped, dropped, and prayed: *Lord, help me!*

The truth soothed my mind: REST—remember, exalt, surrender, trust. I repeated the acronym, which has become a mantra for me as I battle anxiety. Then I took the following steps:

- I pressed my fingers to my temples, as I often do when a headache strikes, and I spoke to my soul, "Remember."
- Then I lifted my hands in praise and proclaimed, "Exalt."
- Afterward, I bowed my head, placing my palms together, and prayed, "Surrender."
- Then I extended my hands out in front of me, with my palms turned upward toward heaven, and confessed, "Trust."

What do I mean by all these gestures and proclamations? For me, they are a gentle reminder of a strategy for spiritual warfare that I have observed all through the Bible. Many people in the Old Testament knew about this approach to entering REST. Moses reminded the children of Israel many times of this truth as he led them out of bondage and through the wilderness. And even Joshua repeated this reminder of God's presence as they entered their promised land of rest.

New Testament believers mirrored their actions through their faith. Jesus showed us this example in the Garden of Gethsemane: "My Father, if there is any way, get me out of this. But please, not what I want. You, what do *you* want?" (Matt. 26:39 *The Message*).

As Jesus faced his impending death,

- He *remembered* his Father's promises to him.
- He *exalted* his Father during his darkest hour.
- He *surrendered* his will.
- He chose to *trust* his Father, taking the steps of faith needed—even though he knew it meant death on a cross.

Then Jesus repeated his prayer, as he continued to struggle with his destiny: "My Father, if there is no other way than this, drinking this cup to the dregs, I'm ready. Do it your way" (Matt. 26:42 *The Message*).

Jesus revealed the supernatural power of God's REST as he remembered, exalted, surrendered to, and trusted his heavenly Father.

One Word

As the rain and the snow come down from heaven, and do not return to it without watering the earth and making it bud and flourish, so that it yields seed for the sower and bread for the eater, so is my word that goes out from my mouth: It will not return to me empty, but will accomplish what I desire and achieve the purpose for which I sent it. (Isa. 55:10–11 NIV)

Maxine, our Bible study teacher, began our new seminary wives' Bible study by announcing that she had prayed for each member of our class that week: "I want to share the scripture that I prayed for each of you individually."

I sat on the edge of my cold metal folding chair as Maxine walked around the classroom. One by one, she gave each of us a narrow strip of paper. She smiled as she extended her gifts, offering her prayers.

I glanced around the room, noticing others curiously unfolding their notes.

I bowed my head and read these poignant words silently: "Yes, my soul, find rest in God; my hope comes from him. Truly he is my rock and my salvation; he is my fortress, I will not be shaken" (Ps. 62:5–6 NIV).

As I soaked in the passage, the penetrating words occupied all my thoughts. *What does this scripture mean? And how does it apply to my life?*

Then my focus returned to Maxine. *How exactly do you "pray a scripture"? And how did she choose the scripture she prayed for me?* The thought that God would speak to someone about an individual was a completely new idea to me. *Does God really speak to people? And if he did, why would he speak to Maxine about me?*

I had never experienced a genuine conversation with God. *How can I hear from the God of the universe? Does he have an audible voice? And does he require some special connection or circumstances to hear him?*

The passage, torn from Maxine's personal prayer journal, tugged on my heartstrings. Her simple prayer revealed my doubts about my personal relationship with God, along with other restless feelings about my life.

When I returned home from church that day, I revisited Maxine's note. And I turned to the scripture in my Bible to see if I could understand why this verse so intrigued me.

> *Yes, my soul, find rest in God;*
> *my hope comes from him.*
> *Truly he is my rock and my salvation;*
> *he is my fortress, I will not be shaken.*
> *My salvation and my honor depend on God;*
> *he is my mighty rock, my refuge.*
> *Trust in him at all times, you people;*
> *pour out your hearts to him,*
> *for God is our refuge. (Ps. 62:5–8 NIV)*

As I considered the words again, I noticed more promises—hope, salvation, protection, acceptance, and rest.

Rest? I didn't know what that scripture meant, but I knew that I had been restless for a long time. I couldn't remember the last time I'd had a full night's sleep, so I knew I needed some rest. But I didn't know how to "find rest in God." *What does that even mean?*

I thought of Maxine—I didn't know her very well. I'd just been attending her class on Sunday mornings for a few weeks. *Did she know about the struggles I'd been going through? I just met her.* I wondered if anyone else could see behind my mask.

Then my thoughts turned to God. *Did he really impress her to focus on this scripture as she prayed for me? Is he even aware of my problems?*

A feeling of hope came as I meditated on the words. The promises soothed my wounded heart. So I tucked the note inside a small pocket in the cover of my Bible for safekeeping.

After I received this unexpected and compelling gift from God's Word, I began to ask God for the rest he promised. And I also responded to my nagging thoughts about my faith in a new way. Even though I had attended church all my life, I didn't know how to apply the stories in the Bible to my life.

Could I control my emotional reactions to all my worries? For the first time, I became aware that in every situation in life, there is moment of choice where I can choose to believe the truth in God's Word or submit to my negative thoughts. And in that very moment, I chose to believe that God's Word held the answers to my problems.

Recognizing that moment of decision proved an important step for me; it helped me begin to break my habits of worrying and focusing on the wrong things. When negative thoughts resurfaced, I whispered a prayer about my worries to God. And hope returned for a moment, until my circumstances distracted me away from the truth again.

As I confessed my concerns, I sensed assurance that God had been listening. When I meditated on God's promises, my heart overflowed with gratitude, cooling the heat of my doubt and distress.

Then I searched for answers to more of the mysteries of life in God's Word, hoping to find solutions for my other problems and reclaim my sanity.

Years later, after life delivered many unexpected, disturbing blows, I remembered those defining *Words That Change Everything* and guided the path of my faith with God's promise of rest.

I also never lost sight of the hope that Maxine offered in her prayer for me. I knew that God's Word held the keys to my contentment and true rest.

Word Power

Words are powerful; take them seriously (Matt. 12:36 The Message)

One time, while posting on a friend's blog, I noticed that I had overlooked a serious typo. Instead of the word "power," I had typed "poser." A minor mistake? Not for a writer! And especially not in this case!

My tiny error distorted the entire significance of this scripture: "But we have this treasure in jars of clay to show that this all-surpassing power is from God and not from us" (2 Cor. 4:7 NIV).

One little word shifted my focus and the potential attention of my readers. All I could see was my mistake. I lost sight of the message and power of God's Word. And my readers may have missed the entire point of my comment.

How many times do we let one little word spoil things for us? We speak a single word of profanity in the heat of an argument, or we whisper a little white lie as we try to cover up a mistake.

We often regret the unexpected consequences that result from our words. A negative comment or careless thought voiced in frustration or anger can blind us from seeing God's blessings in a situation.

As a writer, I cringe when I discover one insignificant word choice that turns a powerful point into a grammatical disaster. And I wince when I read an offensive term that will repel an audience of would-be readers.

As a writing instructor, I notice many students resisting the editing process. They focus on the goal of finishing their writing task instead of fine-tuning their grammar and mechanics. They get offended if anyone calls attention to one tiny mistake or unclear point or if someone suggests a significant but meaningful change. Then they get angry or depressed when they receive a lower grade for their work or the piece is rejected for publication.

As a follower of Christ, I've also experienced the power of God's Word. One word of encouragement can pull me out of the deepest pit of despair. A single promise from God's Word can offer hope to me when my circumstances seem overwhelming. My simple confession of faith can produce peace in my heart and mind, "which exceeds anything [I] can understand" (Phil. 4:7 NLT).

So does one little word matter? God's Word answers this question: "In the beginning was the Word, and the Word was with God, and the Word was God" (John 1:1 NIV).

Examining REST

As we examine REST in the next few chapters, we will see God's people find REST in the middle of battles, storms, times of waiting, and other fearful situations. We will also review the actions of several women who found the "secret of contentment" and REST as they claimed their promised land. And I will share a few personal experiences.

Claiming our promised land requires a strategic battle plan to conquer the enemies of our soul. So prepare to also put on your armor as we learn to REST in God's peace. In the next chapter, we'll focus on the first word in the REST acronym—*remember*.

Remember

Focusing on God's Presence

The Lord is near. (Phil. 4:5 NIV)

M y sister Cathy and I stayed at the hospital with Mother for several days while her doctors ran tests, frustrated by their inability to accurately diagnose Mother's illness. At that time, they had ruled out every known malady except a rare, fatal brain disorder called Creutzfeldt-Jakob Disease (CJD).

After Mother's internist explained some of the horrible symptoms and prognosis of that disease, he added, "But we can't be sure until her autopsy."

"Her autopsy? You mean you can't determine what she has until after her death?"

"Yes, I'm afraid that we've done all we can do at this point. We'll keep her as comfortable as possible."

According to the CJD Foundation's online fact sheet, "Diagnosis of CJD is very difficult and is often made from clinical observation and/or process of elimination of other diseases. The diagnosis of CJD can only be confirmed through a brain biopsy or autopsy."[7]

What is CJD? Although we were told that Mother might have the "human form of mad cow disease," we discovered from the online CJD fact sheet that CJD is *not* "mad cow disease." Bovine spongiform encephalopathy (BSE), the technical term for mad cow disease, occurs only in cows.

Cathy and I looked at each other in disbelief. We didn't know what to say as we stood at Mother's bedside. Silent and still, Mother appeared to be in shock. She didn't seem to comprehend the doctor's statement. She escaped reality and drifted into some unknown world most of the time.

Mother left the hospital after a few days, but as we waited for the test results, more disturbing symptoms emerged. For the next few weeks, we observed Mother's health quickly deteriorate and frantically continued to search for more information about this "incurable disease" that was taking our mother's life.

The doctor suspected Mother had sporadic CJD (sCJD), as described online in the CJD Foundation Fact Sheet:

> In the early stages of the disease, CJD patients may exhibit failing memory, behavior changes, impaired coordination and/or visual disturbances. As the illness progresses, mental deterioration becomes more pronounced, and involuntary movements, blindness, weakness of extremities, and, ultimately, coma may occur. sCJD [sporadic CJD] usually occurs later in life and typically leads to death within a few weeks or months to one year following the onset of symptoms.

In fact, all the information I discovered about CJD did not calm me—it only heightened my worries and my fears. It made me physically ill just thinking about Mother's illness—particularly what it was doing to her brain. When we were told that infected beef was thought to be the cause of the variant form of CJD (vCJD) in humans (another possible diagnosis for Mother), I couldn't stand the thought of eating beef for fear of contracting that horrible disease. I wondered, *Is it genetic? Have we exposed ourselves by caring for Mother? Is it even safe to eat beef or wild game at all?*

Taking care of Mother's physical needs threatened us all. The medical community cautioned us about exposure to the disease, insisting we wear surgical gloves to care for her. Their feeble attempts to assure us of our safety failed, and the threat of exposure loomed over our heads like a medieval plague.

I found myself ill-equipped for the caregiver role. The sights, smells, and sounds associated with medical procedures nauseated me, and the speculation, worry, and grief we experienced in waiting rooms left me in an ongoing state of anxiety.

When the doctors released Mother to her home under hospice care, I struggled with the idea of leaving her side. *How could I leave Mother at a time like this? And how could I abandon my siblings, neglecting my share of the responsibility for Mother's care?*

I had planned a quick visit to my hometown for my niece's wedding. My daughter, Tara, who was well into her pregnancy with her third son, accompanied me with her lively toddler. After a hard, seven-hour drive to Arkansas, I quickly returned to Texas to help care for Mother.

Hiding Place

For you are my hiding place; you protect me from trouble.
You surround me with songs of victory. (Ps. 32:7 NLT)

Driving back to Texas, I thought about the upcoming changing seasons. And I remembered an important lesson I'd learned one windy day the previous fall.

As the autumn winds rushed through the oak trees in our backyard, depositing the leaves across our property, Dan mentioned that we probably wouldn't see any squirrels playing in the trees that day. "In fact, if the wind is blowing when you want to go squirrel hunting, you might as well stay home," he said. "A squirrel won't move too far from the nest on windy days, so you'll have a hard time bagging any."

A squirrel knows to be still and rest on windy days—not because he's tired, but because that is when he is most vulnerable to predators. When the wind is blowing, a squirrel can't hear the other sounds around him; his instincts are blurred by the wind-tossed branches and leaves rustling.

Dan said the same rule applies to deer hunting in our part of the state. Deer don't move around much when the elements prevent them from using their God-given senses to protect them from predators.

I've lived in Texas or Arkansas all my life, and we've survived many storms, tornadoes, and hurricanes. It's difficult to be ready for any kind of storm. I've run away from hurricanes, and I've hidden in our "safe place" during a tornado. But I can't stop storms from coming my way. When a storm swirls all around me, I just need to be still and wait. Sailors also know not to sail into a storm.

I rely on this truth when I'm experiencing a serious setback, paralyzing problems, chaotic confusion, or even an incurable disease. I know that I can't stop the threat of storms, but I can choose a safe hiding place.

Locating a place to rest in the storms of life isn't always easy. I'm tempted to keep trying to protect myself, but God reminds me that he is my true refuge during those times. And I've found his shelter to be a safe place during those threatening days.

Those who live in the shelter of the Most High
will find rest in the shadow of the Almighty.

This I declare about the Lord:
He alone is my refuge, my place of safety;
*   he is my God, and I trust him. (Ps. 91:1–2 NLT)*

Dwelling on the promises in God's Word became a shelter for my heart and mind. As my thoughts drifted back to Mother's impossible situation, I knew I needed something to derail me from my worries.

Another promise of God's faithfulness comes from Psalms 37: "I was young and now I am old, yet I have never seen the righteous forsaken or their children begging bread" (Ps. 37:25 NIV).

Searching for Hope

What do you do when you feel like your world is crashing in around you and your faith fails you?

As I faced the troubling circumstances around my mother's illness, the red flags of worry flapped violently overhead again. And when I looked for evidence of God's intervention and activity, I could not always find it.

I did not sense his peace at all as fear invaded my heart. So while we awaited the test results, I tried to dismiss the tormenting thoughts without much success.

As I searched for help in the Bible, I read about the wilderness journey of the children of Israel again. I considered the struggle Moses experienced as he accepted God's call to lead his people out of the bondage of slavery in Egypt. But deliverance didn't come easy for them—nor did it come as they expected.

Even after Israel escaped Egypt's bondage, they had to pass through the Red Sea before they would get a glimpse of God's promised land of rest. In fact, they faced forty years of trouble in the wilderness after their release from slavery. Even then, most of them never entered because of their fear, doubt, and unbelief.

Could this be true of Jesus's followers today? Do we have to face even more trouble after we discover Christ, as he begins to lead us out of our sinful ways? How long will we wander around in our wilderness of fear, doubt, and unbelief? Can we enter our land of rest here on earth, or is that just a hope of heaven for the believer?

Jesus spoke clearly to these questions with his disciples, saying, "In this world you will have trouble . . . But take heart! I have overcome the world" (John 16:33 NIV).

Red Flags at the Red Sea

Was it not you who dried up the sea, the waters of the
great deep, who made a road in the depths of the sea so
that the redeemed might cross over? (Isa. 51:10 NIV)

After a fearful deliverance process, the children of Israel faced additional obstacles as they pursued their promised land—the Red Sea in front of them, immovable mountains on both sides, and their oppressors pursuing them (Exod. 14).

As Israel confronted more obstacles, "[t]hey were terrified and cried out to the Lord," complaining to Moses, their spiritual leader, "It would have been better for us to serve the Egyptians than to die in the desert!" (Exod. 14:10–12 NIV).

And Moses remembered God's promise to be with them:

> "Do not be afraid. Stand firm and you will see the deliv-
> erance the Lord will bring you today. The Egyptians you
> see today you will never see again. The Lord will fight
> for you; you need only to be still." (Exod. 14:13–14 NIV)

As they remembered God's presence, exalted his promises over their situation, and surrendered their lives to him, trusting his leadership, they experienced God's miraculous deliverance again.

Did you identify the red flags in that story? What caused all their emotional responses? Here, we can identify the following contributing factors:

- Red Sea in front of them
- Immovable mountains on both sides
- Oppressors pursuing them

Once again, we observe God choosing our natural emotional responses to get our attention. God wanted his people to call on him for help—to remember that he was with them. He can move mountains, oceans, rivers, and oppressors with the power of his Word.

What did they do to survive the life-threatening events? They embraced the power of REST as they remembered, exalted, surrendered, and trusted the Lord. As they began to walk by faith, God removed all the obstacles in their path as they journeyed to their promised land.

Why all the drama? Why wait until the last possible minute to deliver them? I'm not sure we will ever answer all the "why" questions in our lifetime. All I know—God had a plan. And the last minute drama made his deliverance appear even more miraculous.

Personal Application

Have you ever faced an impossible task, surrounded by debilitating fear and pursued by your past sins?

At times, I've resisted God's guidance, doubting the direction that I've sensed he'd given me, even after seeking him diligently. Many times, after overcoming one challenge, another unexpected difficulty came up. Then my doubts increased. That seems to be a pattern in life. God guides me through a struggle, only for another one to appear around the corner.

But like Moses, whenever we encounter a crisis of belief and doubt God, we are at a critical crossroads. We can step forward, trusting him and his timing, or we can look at ourselves and trust our emotions.

God has promised to give us the strength to complete the work that he's given us. When we rely on him, we can enter our "promised land."

Getting through Red Sea Experiences

I've faced seemingly impossible tasks, constant worries, and sinful strongholds. In fact, I face them every time I approach a decision in my faith walk.

God doesn't always deliver me *from* my troubles. Many times, deliverance comes *through* my troubles—and often at the last minute. Red Sea obstacles always appear impossible. And I often complain, "Lord, if you don't come through, I'm not going to make it."

When my dad was terminally ill, I asked God to heal him from cancer. But God delivered Dad *through* his death, not *from* it. Eventually, I realized that my dad entered heaven with no more pain, sickness, or death. Yet I never have overcome my sadness; even though it's been four decades since his death, I still miss him every day.

Yet God did give me the grace to get through it. And I sensed God's peace even when I walked through the dark valley of death with Dad:

> Even when I walk through the darkest valley, I will not
> be afraid, for you are close beside me. Your rod and your
> staff protect and comfort me. (Ps. 23:4 NLT)

Through Dad's death, God brought several of my family members into a closer relationship with each other and with him. For me, his death raised some emotional red flags that I'd never seen, leading me to seek answers from God in my desperation. I had never faced a devastating loss before that time in my life.

But God redeemed those hard days as I searched for the truth about heaven. I found out God loves and accepts me just as I am because of what Jesus did on the cross, not because of what I have or have not done.

Now I know for certain the Holy Spirit lives in me, and he will guide me through impossible tasks, immovable mountains, and any wickedness I might encounter.

When I lost my earthly father, I reached out for a relationship with my heavenly Father. He promised to never leave me for any reason—even death.

> If you love me, show it by doing what I've told you. I will
> talk to the Father, and he'll provide you another Friend
> so that you will always have someone with you. This
> Friend is the Spirit of Truth. The godless world can't take
> him in because it doesn't have eyes to see him, doesn't
> know what to look for. But you know him already
> because he has been staying with you, and will even be
> *in* you! (John 14:15–17 *The Message*)

So when another storm blew in, threatening my mother's life, I found strength in the knowledge that I had already survived other spiritual crises. And while I never sensed total peace about my dad's death, I knew that with the Lord's help I would survive the crisis with Mother.

At times, my emotions tempt me to become angry with everyone—including God. And most of these times my frustration compounds because I don't understand why things are happening. I needed to blame someone—even God. I grieved over the loss of loved ones that I cherished. Often I even tried to avert the crisis. But even when I did all I could do, it still happened.

I know that bad things happen to everyone in time. But the Lord promises to be with us, even in our pain, anger, and unbelief. And he promised,

> When the Spirit of truth comes, he will guide you into all truth. He will not speak on his own but will tell you what he has heard. He will tell you about the future. (John 16:13 NLT)

You may be walking in deep valleys of despair that you will never totally get over, and you may also be angry with God. I pray God's promises will encourage you as you remember that he is always with you.

Jesus comforted his disciples with these words:

> "I have told you all this so that you may have peace in me. Here on earth you will have many trials and sorrows. But take heart, because I have overcome the world." (John 16:33 NLT)

You may not think you can trust God. Or you might not even believe God exists. I hope you will remember this truth in God's Word. If you seek him, you can find him:

> So let God work his will in you. Yell a loud *no* to the Devil and watch him scamper. Say a quiet *yes* to God and he'll be there in no time. (Jas. 4:8 *The Message*)

The Bible offers this promise: "[Y]ou will know the truth . . . the truth will set you free" (John 8:32 NIV).

Remembering God's Promises

In his sermon "Israel at the Red Sea," Reverend C. H. Spurgeon points out three major difficulties that God's people face:[8]

- The great trials in front of them

- The sins pursuing them
- Their weak faith

Yet the children of Israel had a strong spiritual leader who reminded them of the powerful, protective care of God and his covenant relationship with them.

Spurgeon reminds us that although God's Word does promise that his people will have trouble, he also promises to be with them as their faith is tested with the divine purpose of drawing them into a deeper relationship with him.

Spurgeon also mentioned the hopeless state of unconverted souls. They will face their Red Seas alone, without a Savior—finding no hope, peace, deliverance, eternal life, or rest at the end of their trials.

Jesus promised that his followers would receive the gift of the Holy Spirit to help them find God's truth. "But when he, the Spirit of truth, comes, he will guide you into all the truth. He will not speak on his own; he will speak only what he hears, and he will tell you what is yet to come" (John 16:13 NIV).

The Spirit will help us properly interpret God's Word and apply the scriptures to our lives. But first, we must *ask*.

> For everyone who asks, receives. Everyone who seeks, finds. And to everyone who knocks, the door will be opened. (Luke 11:10 NLT)

> But when you ask, you must believe and not doubt, because the one who doubts is like a wave of the sea, blown and tossed by the wind. (James 1:6 NIV)

Reflecting on God's Presence

When we look back at Moses and the children of Israel and their bouts with doubt and unbelief, we may wonder how they could have forgotten about God's power, especially since he provided visible signs of his presence—the cloud by day and the fire by night. But they continued to struggle with their faith, held captive by fear.

God revealed his powerful presence on earth again when he sent his Son, Jesus. He also wanted to show the extent of his love by sending Jesus to serve as a living sacrifice for the sins of mankind.

As Jesus's ministry on earth drew near the end, he explained to his followers that in order for his Spirit to remain with them, he would have to leave. Although the disciples didn't understand it at the time of Jesus's death, later God introduced his Holy Spirit, who came to live within each believer.

God also promises to reveal the power of his presence and his Word today through the ministry of the Holy Spirit. The Holy Spirit testifies to God's presence here on earth—now living in all believers. And God continues to remind us as believers about the power of his presence.

Often we fail to acknowledge the presence of the Holy Spirit in us when we focus on our circumstances. Yet when we are reminded that his Spirit lives in us, we can exalt his name and his Word, surrender our worries, and trust him to take care of us.

I wish I would remember to REST every time I meet worry face to face, but I don't. Even now, there is still worry in my life. Yet I know that God promises to always be with me and will take care of my concerns as I REST in him.

Remember

Jesus promised, "I'll be with you as you do this, day after day after day, right up to the end of the age" (Matt. 28:20 *The Message*).

> *On your feet now—applaud GOD!*
> *Bring a gift of laughter,*
> *sing yourselves into his presence.*

Know this: GOD is God, and God, GOD.
He made us; we didn't make him.
We're his people, his well-tended sheep.

Enter with the password: "Thank you!"
Make yourselves at home, talking praise.
Thank him. Worship him. (Ps. 100:1–4 The Message*)*

Exalt

Experiencing the Power of Praise

Do not be anxious about anything, but in every situation,
by prayer and petition, with thanksgiving,
present your requests to God. (Phil. 4:6 NIV)

Loud wails and intense sobbing greeted me as I walked up the sidewalk toward my mother's front door. I recognized Mother's voice, so I pushed the door open and rushed in without knocking.

I witnessed something I had never seen before with my mother—hysteria, an uncontrollable emotional breakdown.

When I left her home a few days earlier, she didn't seem to be in distress; perhaps unaware of the reality of her failing health. I asked myself, *Why is she crying? Is she experiencing physical pain? Grief? Anger?*

Mother covered her face with her hands as she leaned forward in her overstuffed rocking chair. My sister Cathy sat close by—tissues in hand—ready to provide whatever comfort Mother would accept.

Cathy glanced up at me as I walked in, frowning and shrugging her shoulders as our eyes met.

"Mother, I'm home!" Although this house was not my home any longer, I often greeted Mother with those words. But my words did not provide any comfort for Mother, as I hurried across the room and embraced her.

"She's been like this all day," Cathy explained as she fought back her tears.

Confusion and darkness appeared to rule Mother's thoughts as she battled a disease that was destroying her mind. And as I knelt down to hug her, she melted into my arms.

"Mother, are you afraid of dying?" I felt her fear spreading over all of us.

"No . . . of living!"

Mother's Salvation Experience

I knew Mother was confident that she would experience eternal life in heaven after death. She had called me several years earlier to tell me about her own life-changing experience during heart surgery.

"I get it now, Karen! When I died on the operating table, I knew I was going to hell!"

"What? You died?" I listened closely as Mother detailed her terrifying experience.

"I saw horrible creatures all around me as I fell into a pitch black tunnel."

I silently listened and attempted to piece together the situation. *Did she have a hallucination? A nightmare? A heavenly vision?*

"Suddenly I sensed God calling me back to life—like a beam of light pulling me up from the darkness."

Speechless, I listened as Mother described coming back to life.

"I saw shattered pieces of a twisted ladder being drawn together and rebuilt by some magnetic force." She described the twisted ladder as "glowing" and "brightly colored."

"Wow! Like human DNA!" As Mother spoke, I recalled a photo in a science magazine I had seen illustrating a scientific rendering of human DNA.[9]

"What is DNA?"

I told Mother what little I knew about DNA, but it amazed me that she had never heard of it. Yet her illustration vividly mirrored the DNA sketch.

As I continued to listen to Mother's story, my mind fast-forwarded, trying to comprehend what had happened. *Was it a near-death experience? Or mother's salvation? Or both?*

"I couldn't wait to tell you, Karen. Now I understand what you've been telling me about having a personal relationship with Jesus. God gave me another chance to put my faith in him."

As soon as Mother recovered from the surgery, she confessed her faith to her pastor and requested baptism at her church. She had reached out to Jesus to save her from a horrible eternity, and he gave her a second chance. Like me, she had known all about Jesus, but she had never asked him to forgive her, receiving the promise of eternal life.

Even though rejection and judgment of my faith is still painful, Mother's faith story reinforced my faith in God and prepared me for a crisis that would come later.

Seeking the truth in God's Word to resolve my doubts and fears strengthened my faith. Now I never hesitate telling my faith story, encouraging listeners to write down the stories that matter most to them.

Overwhelming Fears

As Mother began to comprehend that her illness might be fatal, her fears overwhelmed her. Even though she had hope for her eternal life, the fears caused by her symptoms weighed heavily on her mind and emotions.

I wondered, *Will Mother find comfort and freedom from her fears this time? Will she trust the Lord to be with her as she walks through this dark valley and possibly faces her own death?*

Then my thoughts turned inward. *How can I find rest and freedom from my fears and worries? Can I trust the Lord to be with me as I face this horrible illness with Mother?*

I knew I needed to affirm my faith instead of expressing my doubts and fears to Mother. But what could I say to her? What could I do to offer her hope and support?

What could I say to my family members that would help them carry the heavy burden of caring for Mother?

What could I speak to my own soul? And how could I express my thoughts to God? And what could I do to calm down and respond to this unexpected dilemma?

After a few days, Mother withdrew and rarely spoke at all. But as we helped care for her, God continued to provide all that we needed.

Sitting near Mother on her sofa one day, I noticed her eyes fixed on the high ceiling in her townhouse living room. "What do you see, Mother?"

"Heaven," she responded without changing her expression.

Shocked by her answer, I asked, "What does it look like?"

"Huge," she sighed.

What a perfect description of heaven, I thought. *Thank You, Lord. I know you are preparing a place for Mother right now, just as you promised.*

A promise from John 14:2 brought peace to my grieving heart. "My Father's house has many rooms; if that were not so, would I have told you that I am going there to prepare a place for you?" (NIV).

Lord, thank you for giving Mother this vision of heaven to ease her tormented mind.

During the following days, Mother lost her ability to communicate. And as the end of her life drew near, we read passages from the Bible to her about heaven. I sang songs about heaven to Mother, along with my brother, Tommy, and my two sisters, Cathy and Leslea. Speaking God's truth to our souls, singing about heaven, and praying together for Mother brought peace and unity to our family.

Offering the Sacrifice of Praise

"Through Jesus, therefore, let us continually offer to God a sacrifice of praise—the fruit of lips that openly profess his name." (Heb. 13:15 NIV)

During Mother's illness, I used praise strategies that had strengthened me during earlier family crises. I found solace in old church hymns and choruses, such as "On Jordan's Stormy Banks I Stand," written by Samuel Stennett in 1787:[10]

On Jordan's stormy banks I stand,
And cast a wishful eye
To Canaan's fair and happy land,
Where my possessions lie.

I am bound for the promised land,
I am bound for the promised land;
Oh who will come and go with me?
I am bound for the promised land.

Since our family name is Jordan, this hymn intrigued me during those hard days and nights. I wondered if I was standing on my own "stormy banks," longing for my promised land.

When I felt despair and grief weighing me down, I reminded myself that I could remove the heavy cloak of worry by listening to worshipful music. Isaiah 61:3 encourages us that God has provided "for those who grieve . . . a crown of beauty instead of ashes, the oil of joy instead of mourning, and a garment of praise instead of a spirit of despair" (NIV).

As I learned more about the power of music and praise, I remembered hearing a man who had been involved in the secular music industry tell his story of visiting a church service for the first time. As the music began to play, he whispered to his wife, "Cool mood music."

As a musician, he recognized the value and power of using music to set the mood for worship within that religious setting, even though he had never attended church.

I laughed as I heard his story. But I understood that I often set the mood in my home in the same way. Listening to blues music made me feel depressed or sad. When I needed to clean my house, I tuned into my upbeat radio station. But when I encountered the power of praise, I began to listen to positive and encouraging Christian music all the time. Praise seemed to drive away my feelings of loneliness and depression.

I learned more about praise from a series of messages delivered by Jack Taylor, who became our pastor. He also taught me that there are at least two types of people in a congregation—those who "need to minister" and those who "need to be ministered to." So when I didn't want to engage in the worship, it became clear which group I fit into that day. When I need emotional healing, I have nothing to offer anyone.

Many times during trials in my life, God has used praise and worship music to soothe my broken heart. I believe that songs of praise allow us to completely envelop ourselves in awe at the wonder of God's presence. I feel that sometimes it is as simple as calling on his name. So in an effort to recall some of the names of God, I wrote these lyrics to speak to my soul:

Who He Is
Jehovah, "I am who I am"

You are my faithful provider, **Jehovah-Jireh**, *you are to me*
The all and powerful healer, **Jehovah-Rophe**, *eternally*
Jehovah-Nissis, *you are my banner, my certain victory*
Jehovah-M'Kaddesh, *sanctifier, to make righteous or holy*

I know you are **Jehovah-Shalom**, *the God of Peace,*
     you will bless
Jehovah-Tsidkenu, *you are my righteousness*
Jehovah-Rohi, *you are my shepherd, my guide everywhere*
Jehovah-Shammah, *faithful companion,*
     you are the Lord who is always there

You are my provider, my healer, my banner, my sanctifier
You are my peace, my righteousness, my shepherd,
     who is always there[11]

I did not want to forget what God was teaching me about the power of his name through praise, so I wrote down my thoughts in rhyme, with a unique beat and tune. And I penned short, free-verse poetry, which, for me, was the fastest and simplest way to record it.

Some nights, I would wake up hearing other tunes and lyrics playing in my mind, forcing me to get up and write them down. Those late-night songwriting episodes came frequently during that season of my life.

These are the specific verses that I chose to help me remember the names of God:

- Jehovah: "I AM WHO I AM" (Exod. 3:14 NIV)
- Jehovah-Jireh: "The LORD Will Provide" (Gen. 22:14 NIV)

- Jehovah-Rophe: "I am the LORD, who heals you" (Exod. 15:26 NIV)
- Jehovah-Nissis: "The LORD is my Banner" (Exod. 17:15 NIV)
- Jehovah-M'Kaddesh: "I am the LORD, who makes you holy" (Lev. 20:8 NIV)
- Jehovah-Shalom: "The LORD Is Peace" (Judg. 6:24 NIV)
- Jehovah-Tsidkenu: "The LORD Our Righteous Savior" (Jer. 23:6 NIV)
- Jehovah-Rohi: "The LORD is my shepherd" (Ps. 23:1 NIV)
- Jehovah-Shammah: "THE LORD IS THERE" (Ezek. 48:35 NIV)

Even after embracing the power of praise, I still didn't feel like worshipping the Lord at times. So I played praise music when I needed to get my mind off my worries and refocus on God's promises.

While taking care of my mother, I knew that listening to uplifting songs and music would help me and possibly bring some joy to her in her helpless state.

Not only did I discover many scriptures that encouraged and demonstrated praise, I found that praise produced the power to replace my negative thoughts.

Some mornings, a familiar chorus would interrupt my thoughts, like "Spirit Song" by John Wimber. At other times, a scripture song would chase away my blues. "My Peace" by Keith Routledge helped me focus on the spiritual truth found in John 14:27: "Peace I leave with you; my peace I give you. I do not give to you as the world gives. Do not let your hearts be troubled and do not be afraid" (NIV).

Even when I did not feel like it—especially then—I would turn on praise music. It was difficult at first. Sometimes it was through a clenched jaw, but I would choose to enter into private worship and praise.

The battle within me raged on Sunday mornings. Even when I could attend church, I did not always want to go. And I especially did not want to sing. But I went, and I sang. Many times I just sat with my eyes shut, bathed by the worship of those around me.

During this trying time, whenever worry would visit my thoughts, some of the song lyrics or a scripture would come to mind and defeat it. Many mornings, I would play simple choruses on my piano to refocus my anxious thoughts. One of my favorites, "Cares Chorus" by Kelly Willard, reminded me of this promise from God's Word: "Give all your worries and cares to God, for he cares about you" (1 Peter 5:7 NLT).

I believe in the power of speaking God's Word and his name over my problems. And as I experience REST, God's promises serve as a foundation for my prayers.

For instance, as I dealt with Mother's illness, I would speak God's promises to my soul—even aloud at times. And I would turn to GraceTalk, reminding myself to REST whenever I needed it:

- *Remember*, the Lord is always near.
- I choose to *exalt* your name, Jehovah Jireh; I thank you for your promise to provide all I need according to your riches in Christ Jesus.
- Lord, I choose to *surrender* my worries to you.
- And I *trust* that you will complete the work in me that you promised.

When darkness and depression would try to settle in, often I would choose to sit at my piano and pick out one of the tunes the Lord had given me. I penned these lyrics in my journal during those hours:

Offer to him a sacrifice of praise whenever
the feeling is not there.
He will supply all that you need—his peace,
his love, and his care.
Offer to him your sacrifice, your broken

and humble heart.
Call upon him and offer your praise,
even when you are falling apart.

I offer to you a sacrifice of praise,
even though the feeling is not there.
I know you'll supply all I need—your peace,
your love, and your care.
I offer to you my sacrifice, humbly, with a broken heart.
In calling on you, I offer my praise;
this praise will be a new start.[12]

"One Thing" Needed

"Martha, Martha," the Lord answered, "you are worried
and upset about many things, but few things are needed—
or indeed only one. Mary has chosen what is better, and it
will not be taken away from her." (Luke 10:41–42 NIV)

When I read the account of Martha complaining to Jesus about
Mary, I usually focus on Martha's complaints and Jesus's reactions.
But have you ever considered how Mary must have felt about their
discussion?

Often the two different natures of Martha and Mary seem to
battle for control within me.

The "Mary" part of me desires to focus on Jesus—to meditate on all he's teaching me. I desire a deeper relationship with
him. I want to know him more. I need him to calm all my fears,
answer all my questions, give me direction, and heal my wounds
and afflictions.

I desire to trust him to fight my battles for me. I long to sense
his presence with me all the time. And I want to be able to listen
to his Word and respond in faith and obedience. I hope to feel his
strength in my weakness. I yearn for his guidance when I've lost

my way. I'm desperate for him to pull me up out of the thorny paths of life where I'm struggling with the prickly worries of this world.

Then I hear Martha's voice from behind me, trying to distract me and reminding me of all that needs to be done and what I haven't accomplished. She points out all my weaknesses and brings up my past failures. She complains that I'm not serving the Lord in the way I should. And she always has a better idea of how something should be done.

She accuses me of not taking care of the needs of my family. She reminds me of how much time I'm wasting. She judges my worship as silly and childlike. She tells me that I need to grow up and get busy. She says there are mouths to feed, clothes to wash, dishes to clean, floors to scrub, and "times a-wasting." She points out that my devotion is costing me friends and that others think I'm crazy and lazy.

The sad part about this battle is that Martha is the one who is more like the "old" me than I'd like to admit. Martha reminds me of how I was before Christ (i.e., me BC).

The Lord continues to expose the "Mary" and "Martha" within me with the truth I find in his Word. And I'm finally beginning to believe who I am "in Christ." "This means that anyone who belongs to Christ has become a new person. The old life is gone; a new life has begun!" (2 Cor. 5:17 NLT).

As Mary "sat before the Master, hanging on every word he said," Martha complained to Jesus, wanting Mary to assist her in the kitchen (Luke 10:38–40 *The Message*).

Jesus defended Mary's worship, silencing Martha's accusing voice with his words: "Martha, dear Martha, you're fussing far too much and getting yourself worked up over nothing. One thing only is essential, and Mary has chosen it—it's the main course, and won't be taken from her" (Luke 10:41–42 *The Message*).

The Word of God can set me free from my condemning thoughts and accusations. And for another season, Martha is silenced within me. But the Martha in me always tries to divert my attention, especially from that "one thing"—listening to the Word of God.

How can I repel the attacks of Martha's accusations? The answer lies in my ability to stay focused on the Lord instead of detractors.

As I examine other stories about Mary in the Bible, I see that she had many encounters with Jesus.

In John 11, the Bible records the death and resurrection of Lazarus, the brother of Mary and Martha. When Lazarus died, Mary stayed home while Martha ran to question Jesus. When Martha told Mary that Jesus asked for her, she quickly responded and went to him. Then, as she poured out her broken heart to her Savior, he grieved with her (John 11:17–35).

Jesus wants to carry our burdens. He promises to provide his rest as we give him our burdens:

> Come to me, all of you who are weary and carry heavy
> burdens, and I will give you rest. Take my yoke upon
> you. Let me teach you, because I am humble and gentle
> at heart, and you will find rest for your souls. For my
> yoke is easy to bear, and the burden I give you is light.
> (Matt. 11:28–30 NLT)

In John 12:1–6, we can observe Mary and Martha again, following the resurrection of Lazarus. Martha serves a dinner given in Jesus's honor, this time without complaining about Mary. And Lazarus reclines at the table with Jesus. Mary pours expensive perfume on the feet of Jesus and wipes them with her hair. This time, Judas complains to Jesus about Mary wasting money, which is especially interesting since Judas later betrays Jesus *for* money:

> But Judas Iscariot, the disciple who would soon betray
> him, said, "That perfume was worth a year's wages. It
> should have been sold and the money given to the poor."

> Not that he cared for the poor—he was a thief, and since
> he was in charge of the disciples' money, he often stole
> some for himself. (John 12:4–6 NLT)

Once again, Jesus defends Mary, expressing the important value of her worship. "Leave her alone. She did this in preparation for my burial. You will always have the poor among you, but you will not always have me" (John 12:7–8 NLT).

When I think of Mary breaking her alabaster jar and pouring out the costly oil to anoint Jesus's feet, I see how the Lord used her act of worship to demonstrate to others who he was—to reveal his story.

What a powerful symbol of how his body was broken and poured out to prepare us—the Body of Christ—for his service. The precious, costly oil symbolizes the Holy Spirit: how Jesus had to be broken for his Spirit to be poured out on us.

And I know that the Lord redeems moments when I'm broken and emptied so that his Holy Spirit can flow and comfort me. It's important for me to remember that when I'm feeling the onslaught and grief of life's circumstances, Jesus promises to intervene. When I'm grieving, he speaks to my soul. When I'm broken and emptied of my focus on myself, I can also experience the power of his Holy Spirit in my life.

During these heartbreaking moments, Mary experienced the power of Jesus. She witnessed his intervention, standing in the presence of her accusers, comforting her and raising her brother from the dead. But those were also the very events that changed Mary so she could experience the Lord's power in her weakest moments.

Exalting God's Word

How can we exalt God's Word over our circumstances?

As I exalt God's Word and praise the Lord in any time of trouble, I remember who he is and recall his faithfulness in my life. The supernatural power in our faith stories encourages me to revisit moments when the Lord revealed his power and glory. And as I recount those moments when a storm develops, it allows me to focus on the Lord—the truth.

There are times when I must listen and be filled—not only with food for my body but with power and strength. Speaking God's truth to my soul satisfies my emptiness, gives me strength, and compels me to move forward. This GraceTalk delivers moments of REST as I choose to remember, exalt, surrender, and trust. In the following chapter, I will explore the power of the third component of REST—*surrender.*

Surrender

Raising the White Flag

Do not be anxious about anything, but in every situation,
by prayer and petition, with thanksgiving,
present your requests to God. (Phil. 4:6 NIV)

Guilt hovered over me like a dense fog as I entered Mother's bedroom the morning I had to leave her side for a long-anticipated trip.

How could I interpret the look on Mother's face? Her fixed, sunken eyes pierced my heart with guilt. She knew I was leaving her. Even though she could not speak, feelings of shame and worry accused me as I turned and walked away.

How could I possibly go? But it was impossible to stay.

Searching for Direction

The long weeks of caregiving put all our lives on hold. *How long will this last? Will we ever discover the cause of this horrible disease? When can I go on with my own life?*

Since we didn't know how long Mother would live, we all had to maintain our lives as much as possible. I was already committed to attending my first writers' conference, and my expenses had been provided by funds from my job as writing instructor. I couldn't afford to miss this opportunity. But leaving proved to be one of the hardest decisions I ever had to make.

I'd spent the last five years in college preparing for this moment. My children were grown and on their own now. It was time to pursue my dream of freelance writing. And this proved to be an important step in my journey to publication.

I couldn't complain about my life with Mother on her deathbed. But I also couldn't abandon my own life in the face of our family's tragedy and pain.

I prayed silently to myself. *I want to trust you with Mother's care, Lord. What is the right thing to do? I don't want to be selfish. But I don't want to fail to follow your direction.*

As I continued my dialog with the Lord, I sensed his peace leading me to leave for a few days and attend the writer's conference in New Mexico. I believe that God always leads us with his peace. Colossians 3:15 encourages us, "Let the peace of Christ rule in your hearts, since as members of one body you were called to peace. And be thankful" (NIV).

While this is true, I often find that during troubling days, peace eludes me. In this particular situation, I continued to seek God for answers, and I sensed an urgency to release Mother and trust the Lord to take care of everything in my absence.

Following God often produces resistance from unexpected places, especially when those around us misunderstand our calling and commitment to Christ. And my decision to leave Mother to pursue the training I needed caused me much internal pain.

As I tried to choose the words to tell Mother I needed to leave for a few days, I remembered painful past memories of her using guilt over the years to manipulate me, especially after I moved away from our hometown.

I love my mother dearly, and I would never want to say anything about her that would dishonor or disrespect her. But we always struggled over my resistance to her control. I wasn't the easiest daughter to live with at times. And I regret some of our disagreements and conflicts over the course of our relationship.

I felt that her emotional demands had escalated during the years prior to her illness. I questioned myself and struggled deep inside with many questions: *Had I been too impatient with her? Over the years, should I have taken more time to listen to her and her opinions—solicited or unsolicited?*

When the Lord led Dan and me to attend seminary, we expected that some people would not understand our decision—even Mother. But when I chose to leave Mother for those days, flashbacks of her past accusations and waves of guilt tormented me.

As I prayed about leaving, I had clear direction and peace from God's Word. I knew I needed to prepare for my conference. So without discussing the matter with anyone except Dan, I packed my car to leave early one morning for New Mexico, organizing as many details as I could before my departure.

Leaving

When I walked into Mother's room just before dawn, she glared at me.

Since I was already struggling about leaving, a feeling of nausea washed over me as I prepared to tell Mother I needed to leave for a few days. And the accuser—the enemy of my soul—attacked me with intense fear, guilt, shame, and worry.

"Mother, I told you about the writing conference that I'm going to in New Mexico, right? Well, I need to go home to prepare for that trip."

Mother's eyes didn't blink. Although I knew she couldn't respond, I still thought I needed her approval.

"Can I pray for you again before I leave?" I whispered a prayer. I spoke more words of love and compassion to Mother. Then I kissed her forehead and walked out of the room.

Mother knew I was leaving her. And nothing relieved my guilt at that moment. Even though the past few weeks had placed all our lives on hold, I felt I had no right to complain. *Why am I so caught up and worrying about my hardships? My mother is dying! How long will she suffer like this?*

As I walked out, I looked over my shoulder one last time. She stared at me, and guilt weighed heavy on me as I walked away.

My sister-in-law Penny consoled me as I prepared to leave Mother's home. I waved good-bye to her as she closed the door behind me. My sisters and brother would take care of Mother—I knew that.

But how would they respond to my jumping ship at such a crucial time? My departure placed even more pressure on them and would take more time away from their families.

The walk to my car seemed longer that morning before sunrise, and I sensed the darkness enveloping me. The shadows brought an eerie sense of fear and danger.

I looked around me, and the streets were desolate. As I crossed to enter the parking lot, one of the neighbors turned on their porch light. *Life would go on here without me.*

Opening the rear door of my SUV, I lifted my computer bag and placed it carefully in the corner. I was grateful I could take my work with me.

I had completed my thesis while staying with Mother in the hospital. I read most of it to her there and regretted not reading all of it to her. I felt incredibly fearful about the end of her life.

I slammed the rear door of my vehicle and climbed into the driver's seat. As I put my key in the ignition, I prayed, *Lord, I trust this is the right decision.*

I backed out of my parking space and turned to exit the parking lot. As I passed my Mother's home, I saw Penny peeking through the blinds. She waved good-bye again a final time.

Driving Home

Before boarding my flight to Albuquerque for the conference, I needed to take the long drive home back to Little Rock. I cried when I had traveled a few blocks, releasing all my grief to the Lord.

Once again, I remembered a conflict with Mother just before her illness. One of the hardest things about letting go of someone is the reconciliation it requires. Sometimes it's just impossible. *How could I reconcile with someone who was quickly losing her ability to communicate?*

I dreaded the drive home. Dan usually accompanied me on long trips, but he had been home alone in Little Rock for several weeks. I called to let him know I was on my way home.

"Are you OK?"

"No, not really."

"You're making the right decision, Karen. You've worked hard for this moment. You can't just pass up this opportunity."

"I know. But what if she dies while I'm gone?"

"We'll just have to trust the Lord with that one, Karen."

"I know."

"I'll call you when I'm on my way to work in an hour or so."

"OK."

"I love you, Karen."

"I love you, too."

I placed my cell phone on the console next to me.

Fear continued its attack in the silence. This time, talk radio did not help.

I remembered the CDs I brought along for my trip. I knew that the music could divert my thoughts—at least I hoped it would. My burden for Mother weighed me down, exhausting me from the struggle.

Tears came to my eyes as I listened to "Shackles," by Mary Mary, a song that Mother loved. She told me that the words and the music of that song reminded her of the day the Lord set her free from the fear of death.

Remembering her salvation brought bittersweet tears of joy, since her illness had stolen any hope for her future here on earth. Perhaps this was a merciful way of delivering her from the problems of her life. Now she had no control over her body or mind because her thought process was one of the first things lost with this disease.

I debated every emotional thought the entire drive back to Arkansas. I didn't believe I could handle hours of solitude in the car, but it proved to be exactly what I needed.

As I made the long drive, I realized that I could not win the battle in my heart and mind. I needed time away from Mother's crisis to release my worries and burdens to the Lord. And the journey gave me time to pray, listen, and respond to God privately.

My conference proved to be productive, as I connected with other writers and learned many new things about writing for publication. But before the conference ended, I received a frantic call from my sister Leslea. I needed to leave the conference immediately if I was to see Mother one last time. So I booked the next flight to Texas from Albuquerque, arriving in time to be there before her passing.

Follow Me

Do you often compare yourself to others?

As I read the story of Jesus and his disciples in John 21, I realized that I compare myself to others a lot, especially when I'm frustrated about my own life.

In this story, the disciples had an unsuccessful fishing trip. During the trip, the resurrected Jesus appeared to them on the shore, calling attention to their lack of success: "Fellows, have you caught any fish?" (John 21:5 NLT).

He then instructed them to recast their net: "Throw your net on the right-hand side of the boat and you'll get some!" (John 21:6 NLT).

Once they followed his instructions, they caught so many fish that they couldn't even pull their nets in.

Peter got excited when he realized the man on the shore was the Lord, and he jumped into the water to swim to Jesus. By the time the other disciples made it to shore with the fish in tow, he had prepared a meal for them.

After eating, Jesus had a heart-to-heart talk with Peter, asking him three times, "Do you love me?" (John 21:15–17 NLT).

After Peter's responses, Jesus offered him a glimpse of the future, indicating how Peter's own life would end. It was not an encouraging picture. But "Jesus said this to let him know by what kind of death he would glorify God. Then Jesus told him, 'Follow me.'" (John 21:19 NLT).

How did Peter react? He asked Jesus, "What about him, Lord?" (John 21:20 NLT) and turned around and compared himself to another disciple.

"Jesus replied, 'If I want him to remain alive until I return, what is that to you? As for you, follow me'" (John 21:22 NLT).

White Flag of Surrender

Many times, I become so focused on comparing myself to others I lose sight of who I really am and what's most important. But as a believer in Christ, I know the most important part of my identity is who I am in Christ—rather who I am because of my personal relationship with Jesus.

When I compare myself to others, I become frustrated and worried. Then at other times—like now—I sense that Jesus is telling me to cast my hopes in a different direction. I have to make a choice: Do I worry about what others will think? Or will I choose to follow him instead?

What areas of your life tempt you to not follow Christ? Friends, family, job, money, hobbies, or addictions?

Are you tired of trying to measure up to someone else's standards? Are you ready to become who God created you to be? If you are a Jesus follower, do you really grasp who you are "in Christ"?

Following Christ not only means saying yes to his teachings; I've found it also means saying no to a lot of other things that may be good but keep you distracted from discovering God's best for your life.

While researching this book, many other writing and speaking opportunities emerged for me. But I knew saying "yes" to anything else meant saying "no" to following the Lord's directions for me now and working on this manuscript. Could I do all the things I might want to do and still complete this book by the deadline? For me, the answer was "no." I had to choose to stay focused on my priorities.

Perhaps that's not the best example of surrendering my life to follow Christ, but I sensed God's guidance in writing this book. And saying "no," to me, would be an act of disobedience.

What comes to mind when you see a white flag? Surrender? Truce?

In our culture today, it usually represents losing or conceding defeat. But in God's kingdom, surrender means being liberated— free from the bondage of the enemy of our souls. God's kingdom runs counter to our society—his ways and wisdom are often in conflict, if not diametrically opposed, to the prevailing social and political norms.

"My thoughts are nothing like your thoughts," says the Lord. "And my ways are far beyond anything you could imagine" (Isa. 55:8 NLT).

Do you want to follow Christ? Do you want to be freed from the bondage of your sinful ways? Follow him. Surrender your life to the Word of God—Jesus Christ.

> If any of you wants to be my follower, you must turn from your selfish ways, take up your cross daily, and follow me. If you try to hang on to your life, you will lose it. But if you give up your life for my sake, you will save it. And what do you benefit if you gain the whole world but are yourself lost or destroyed? (Luke 9:23–25 NLT)

chapter 8

Trust

Claiming Our Promised Land

And the peace of God, which transcends all understanding, will guard your hearts and your minds in Christ Jesus. (Phil. 4:7 NIV)

Returning to Mother's home after the writing conference, I walked into her bedroom, and her glazed-over eyes were heartbreaking. I sat down at her side, shocked again by the solemnness of the moment.

A hospital bed had replaced Mother's bedroom furniture in her home, and she had not eaten, spoken, or moved in a few weeks.

Leslea had called me during the third day of the conference. And Mother's quickly failing health prompted me to return a few days ahead of schedule. The hospice nurse had already advised us to call anyone who might want to see Mother before she passed.

When the call came to me in New Mexico, I was in a panic. I didn't know if it was possible to get a flight and make it back before she died. And I didn't even know how to get to the airport.

The shuttles from the conference center were not scheduled that afternoon.

I prayed silently, *Lord, help me! I do not know what to do!*

I called Dan and asked for his help in making arrangements for me to fly back to Texas as soon as possible. As I waited for his call, I spoke to one of the support staff of the Christian Leaders and Speakers Seminars (CLASS) Christian Writers Conference, and I asked for help with transportation to the airport.

Within a few minutes, Dan called with my flight information, and one of the CLASS staff offered to drive me to the airport.

Thank You, Jesus!

I packed and waited for my ride to the airport. I had planned to ride in silence, but instead, my driver shared an account of God's intervention in an impossible situation. With my thoughts totally focused on his miraculous story, the hour-long drive passed quickly. I arrived at the airport with time to spare.

My brother Tommy picked me up at a Houston airport. We drove back to Mother's home without saying much. What could we say that hadn't been said? Our mother was dying, and we were helpless to do anything but wait. We were both exhausted.

Dan drove to Texas from Little Rock, arriving at Mother's home an hour before me. He had called me several times that day to make sure I had made all my connections.

My sister Cathy had been sitting with Mother all night. When I arrived, she had just gone for a shower and fresh clothes.

The hospice nurse sat in the corner of the bedroom with her hands in her lap. The room seemed peaceful in spite of the people going in and out regularly.

As I walked in, my sister Leslea and my sister-in-law Penny rushed over and hugged me tightly. They had been standing at Mother's bedside, struggling over her labored breathing. We all knew that Mother would be gone soon.

I had been there just a few minutes when we saw a change in Mother—her breathing changed dramatically.

Once again, I entered my panic mode—and I phoned Cathy. "Hey, I'm back at Mother's now. And I think you might want to come back as soon as you can." I explained the change in Mother's breathing.

We knew it was the predicted "fish-out-of-water" breathing that we had been advised would happen at the end—it meant death was near.

Cathy arrived within a few minutes to stand at Mother's side with all of us. Mother's husband stood opposite us. Dan and my brother-in-law Richard paced the hallway.

Mother's breathing grew weaker as we placed our hands on her body to pray, releasing her to the Lord. *Was she aware of our presence or our words?*

Then as she drew her last breath, her tight lips opened for a smile, and she voiced her faith, "I'm home!"

Peaceful Homecoming

We all stood in awe of her final words we had witnessed. The room was filled with unexpected hope and joyful surrender.

Everyone knew that Mother had seen heaven by her last words. It was a rare moment of promise and praise.

I looked up into Leslea's eyes, still filled with the awe and excitement of the moment. "Did you hear what she said?" I asked.

Leslea nodded her head in agreement.

I turned to Cathy, and she smiled.

I asked Tommy, "Did you hear?"

"Amazing," someone whispered.

Everyone in the room witnessed a glimpse of heaven at the moment of Mother's death and first step into eternity.

Later, Dan compared the scene to labor in a delivery room. We actually experienced Mother being "birthed into heaven."

This proved to be a moment of blessing for our family in the midst of a great loss.

In my mind's eye, I visualized my dad and other loved ones in heaven, greeting Mother and celebrating her homecoming.

Heavenly Vision

My view of heaven changed because of what I experienced at Mother's death. I was called back to Mother's home before my conference ended, just in time to witness a life-changing miracle.

I couldn't save Mother from her rare disease, but I chose to trust the Lord to walk with us all through it. And God reminded me of many promises like this one in the Psalms: "Even though I walk through the darkest valley, I will not be afraid, for you are close beside me. Your rod and your staff protect and comfort me" (Ps. 23:4 NLT).

I knew that Mother had finally crossed over to her promised land of rest.

Predators of Peace

Have you ever suffered with excruciating pain like a vise clamping its strong, clawlike jaws around your head?

A few years ago, I had to seek medical attention for headaches, but I discovered spiritual insight from God's Word that helped me overcome this bothersome problem.

In the account of Jesus's crucifixion in Matthew, his tormenters "twisted together a crown of thorns and set it on his head" (Matt. 27:29 NIV).

As I meditated on the passage, I identified with the pain inflicted by that crown of thorns, cruelly pressed on Christ's head by his oppressors. Jesus must have endured unbearable misery from the stabbing and relentless pressure of those needlelike, penetrating thorns. But Jesus did not shun his agonizing crown. Instead, he chose to bear its disgrace and anguish. After more humiliating mockery, the soldiers "led him away to crucify him" (Matt. 27:31 NIV).

Jesus chose to submit to torture for a divine purpose. But what was the ultimate impact of his sacrifice? What does the crown of thorns signify in light of his name, "Prince of Peace" (Isa. 9:6 NIV)?

To me, the twisted, blood-spattered crown of thorns that Jesus wore represents a promise of his peace—a spiritual hedge of protection.

The Old Testament uses a hedge to symbolize God's protection from predators. In Job, Satan accuses God of protecting Job with a hedge:

> "Does Job fear God for nothing?" Satan replied. "Have you not put a hedge around him and his household and everything he has? You have blessed the work of his hands, so that his flocks and herds are spread throughout the land. But now stretch out your hand and strike everything he has, and he will surely curse you to your face." (Job 1:9–11 NIV)

In Isaiah, thorn hedges were planted to protect vineyards: "Now I will tell you what I am going to do to my vineyard: I will take away its hedge, and it will be destroyed; I will break down its wall, and it will be trampled" (Isa. 5:5 NIV).

A few years ago, I observed a modern-day "hedge of thorns" on a reality-based television program. The participants, in the African wilderness, built a fence-like structure around their camp by stacking thorny bushes for protection from the lions and jackals in the Serengeti. An infrared camera captured images of the beasts surrounding their manmade fortress—pacing back and forth outside the hedge, huffing and growling, as they searched the night for easy prey.

As the "survivors" crouched in fear around a smoldering campfire, the wild predators prowled—circling, sniffing, and seeking a way through the protective hedge encircling the camp. After hours of stalking, the ravenous beasts finally gave up and retreated into the darkness.

Scripture warns us about spiritual predators: "Stay alert! Watch out for your great enemy, the devil. He prowls around like a roaring lion, looking for someone to devour" (1 Pet. 5:8 NLT).

But how can we protect our minds from intimidating thoughts and accusations—predators of our peace and joy? I believe the Lord wants us to become more than just survivors crouched in fear, consumed by our fear of being devoured.

Paul reminds me in 2 Corinthians that I can't overcome my own debilitating headaches with my own strength or with my own resources. Three times, he begs the Lord to relieve him by removing the "thorn in [his] flesh" (2 Cor. 12:7–8 NIV).

But the Lord responded, "My grace is sufficient for you, for my power is made perfect in weakness" (2 Cor. 12:9 NIV).

Like Paul, I may not find immediate relief from my headaches or any other "thorn in [my] flesh" (2 Cor. 12:7 NIV). But the Lord continues to provide his all-sufficient grace to his followers.

In his book, *The Passion of Jesus Christ*, John Piper speculates on the purpose of Christ's agonizing death: "God meant to show the world that there is no sin and no evil too great that God cannot bring from it everlasting righteousness and joy."[13]

Although we can't completely understand the purpose of Christ's suffering and death this side of heaven, we can find hope in his resurrection and in his Word.

I can't interpret the purpose of Mother's suffering and death either—only that it ultimately transported my mother to her new home in heaven.

For instance, we know that when these bodies of ours are taken down like tents and folded away, they will be replaced by resurrection bodies in heaven—God-made, not handmade—and we'll never have to relocate our "tents" again. Sometimes we can hardly wait to move— and so we cry out in frustration. Compared to what's coming, living conditions around here seem like a stopover in an unfurnished shack, and we're tired of it! We've been given a glimpse of the real thing, our true home, our resurrection bodies! The Spirit of God whets our appetite by giving us a taste of what's ahead. He puts a little of heaven in our hearts so that we'll never settle for less. (2 Cor. 5:1–5 *The Message*)

Getting Ready

"Haven't I commanded you? Strength! Courage!
Don't be timid; don't get discouraged. GOD, your God,
is with you every step you take." (Josh. 1:9 The Message*)*

Standing on the banks of my "Jordan River," I look over to the other side, gazing at my promised land.

Perhaps you've been given a promise that you can visualize for your future. Maybe you've dreamed of a time of rest from your years of work, in retirement.

My husband has been planning his retirement for years. And it seemed like an impossible dream. I recall his fears, doubts, and unbelief—watching other people retire and wondering if it would ever come to pass.

As we drew closer to his announced retirement date, we both became excited about the possibility of it becoming a reality. We thought the battle was almost over.

Then our doubts and fears surfaced again: *Will we have enough money? What about insurance? What obstacles will get in our way between now and then?*

After Dan retired, I considered other challenges: *Will we be able to agree on our plans? Am I going to be able to continue my work as a writer with Dan at home every day? How will his retirement change my life? Will his retirement be what we hoped?*

I sensed the enemy preparing stumbling blocks for us.

Lord, help us!

As I called out to the Lord again, an encouraging promise from God's Word dispelled my fears, "I will be with you; I will never leave you nor forsake you. Be strong and courageous" (Josh. 1:5–6 NIV).

So I inhale slowly—one, two, three, four—and then I exhale, counting to seven. I inhale, counting to eight. As I repeat this focused breathing, trying to avoid another panic attack, I relax.

When I looked up the promise from the book of Joshua, I noticed that the Lord repeats his exhortation twice to Joshua, calling attention to several powerful, yet conditional, promises:

> Be strong and very courageous. Be careful to obey all the law my servant Moses gave you; do not turn from it to the right or to the left, that you may be successful wherever you go. Keep this Book of the Law always on your lips; meditate on it day and night, so that you may be careful to do everything written in it. Then you will be prosperous and successful. Have I not commanded you? Be strong and courageous. Do not be afraid; do not be discouraged, for the LORD your God will be with you wherever you go. (Josh. 1:7–9 NIV)

Remember

After the Lord reminded Joshua of his presence, he instructed him to tell the people to faithfully obey everything he had told them. God also promised to bless their obedience with prosperity and success.

I believe God also promises to bless our obedience. It's tempting to listen to naysayers as I go forward with my writing projects and plans. But I'm reminded once again of God's desire for us to seek him first for direction and to always obey his Word.

Exalt

The Lord also reminded Joshua of the importance of lifting up his Word every day—meditating on his Word day and night.

How can we lift up his Word in our daily lives? To complete a reading of the Bible this year, I'm listening to Brian Hardin's Daily Audio Bible online. At times, when I can't sleep, I use my earphones to listen to God's Word in the stillness of the night. I'm amazed at how scripture calms me as I drift off to sleep.

Surrender

The Lord instructs Joshua to encourage the people to surrender their fears and discouragement, promising he will always be with them.

I depend on the Holy Spirit's promptings when I'm tempted to resume my old mind-set of fear and discouragement. Often a scripture or a song comes to mind, chasing away my fearful thoughts as I focus on God's promises.

Trust

Get your provisions ready. Three days from now you will cross the Jordan here to go in and take possession of the land the LORD your God is giving you for your own . . . The LORD your God will give you rest . . . (but get) ready for battle. (Josh. 1:11–14 NIV)

Just when I think I'm about to occupy my promised land, I read another warning about warfare. *Will I still have battles in my land of rest?*

I think the answer is clear. We must always be aware of our weaknesses, vulnerability, and complete dependence on God. As

Christians, we are called to lead others to claim God's promised land, too.

So get "ready for battle . . . You are to help [others] until the LORD gives them rest, as he has done for you, and until they too have taken possession of the land the LORD your God is giving them" (Josh. 1:14–15 NIV).

Part Three

Retreat

Finding Your Place of REST

When life is heavy and hard to take,

go off by yourself.

Enter the silence. Bow in prayer.

Don't ask questions:

Wait for hope to appear.

(Lam. 3:28–29 *The Message*)

chapter 9

Seek

Searching for Truth

*Seek the Kingdom of God above all else, and live righteously,
and he will give you everything you need. (Matt. 6:33 NLT)*

A few days before I delivered our firstborn, Adam, my mother-in-law died unexpectedly. Her tragic death sent waves of shock and grief throughout our family.

Also, my father-in-law had just been released from the hospital following major surgery. So within days, we felt obligated to abandon our apartment, nursery and all, and move into my father-in-law's home to help him recover.

When my son was born, I came home from the hospital to a strange house with a demanding new baby, without a clue about how to care for him, my recuperating father-in-law, or my grieving husband.

I remember sitting in my mother-in-law's yellow, leather rocker, crying as I tried to rock my newborn son Adam to sleep. I had never faced this kind of crisis before—everything seemed to be caving in on me at once.

As I examined my thoughts, I recalled a verse I found while searching for Adam's name: "For we are God's handiwork, created in Christ Jesus to do good works, which God prepared in advance for us to do" (Eph. 2:10 NIV).

The truth of this memory verse shocked me, so I looked up the scripture in the Bible to see if it was really there. I thought it was probably something I had heard or read many times during my childhood in church. But for some reason, it had just leaped from my subconscious. I had never thought much about the Bible up to that point, although I did attend church regularly. I didn't understand how any of the Bible lessons I was taught as a child could apply to my life.

Yet the scripture washed over me like a gentle rain on that sweltering hot summer day in southeast Texas. Somehow I understood what the passage meant for me. I knew the child I held was a gift to me—God had brought him into my life at this particular time for a reason.

I wish I could say that I continued to seek God for answers to my problems during those early days. But I focused all my attention on trying to survive my new roles as a mom and a wife. My feelings of inadequacy produced negative, self-deprecating thoughts and worries.

Then one morning, I woke up with a shocking thought on my mind: *I haven't even thought about God in months!*

It's odd what you think about when you're not thinking about God. Back then, I thought about myself a lot—my needs and my wants. I thought about how marriage and my son's birth had changed my life. But those changes were not always positive—self-pity and restlessness exploited my emotions.

Once again, I recalled the verse connected to Adam's name. As I read it, I noticed this scripture preceding it:

> For it is by grace you have been saved, through faith—
> and this is not from yourselves, it is the gift of God—not
> by works, so that no one can boast. For we are God's
> handiwork, created in Christ Jesus to do good works,
> which God prepared in advance for us to do. (Eph.
> 2:8–10 NIV)

Grace? Saved? Faith? Works? All these "church" words sounded familiar to me. But motherhood forced me to face my other weaknesses and needs. And I began to wonder what the words I read in the Bible meant for me.

Motherhood Mistakes

What about all my mistakes?

God has covered many of my mistakes through the years. And the Bible offered the peace I needed to get through difficult days and accept my new role of motherhood. But I had made many mistakes in my life. And as a new mother, I began to see how my mistakes were impacting my child.

For instance, I experienced anxiety while taking care of my firstborn. I feared making mistakes that might cause my son harm. Adam always ran a fever with the slightest illness. And he suffered with allergy-related problems, which is rather common in the woods of southeast Texas.

I hate to admit this because it reveals my inept medical knowledge and abilities as a teenage mom, but the first time I tried to use a bulb syringe nasal aspirator to clear his stuffy nose, I thought I had killed him.

We didn't have the Internet back then in the seventies, or I would have consulted a video about how to use the device. All I had were the small-print instructions on the back of the box it came in. And they said to fill the aspirator with warm, soapy water before I used it.

I obviously didn't read the complete directions, because when I squirted that warm, soapy water up Adam's nose, we both came unglued. I'd never seen such gagging and spitting and crying in all my life.

After I finally got us both calmed down, I reread the directions.

I never did admit that incident to anyone—and I can't believe I'm confessing it now. But once again, I beat myself up about my failures and ignorance as a mother. *God, please protect this innocent baby from me! I'm such a terrible mother!*

I wondered if my precious little boy would survive my mothering. Yet, as I sang lullabies to rock Adam to sleep, the words of familiar children's songs I'd learned in church comforted my heart. *Jesus loves the little children. . . .* Somehow I knew Jesus was watching over my son every moment of every day, in spite of my inadequacies.

Do I still make mistakes? You bet. But I try to learn from my errors so I won't keep making them over and over again.

How could God use my mistakes for the good of my child? I'm not sure how, but I know that he has taught me a lot about motherhood from my failures. And he has protected my children in spite of my weaknesses and carelessness.

In fact, Romans 8:28 offers this promise:

> God causes everything (even our mistakes) to work together for the good of those who love God and are called according to his purposes for them. (NLT)

Yes, I still make mistakes. But I've learned from my mishaps and lack of experience. But I also asked for help from those more experienced in parenting—like my own mother and pediatricians. I also saw the importance of connecting with other moms for moral and emotional support, as well as for playtime with our children.

One thing for certain—I now know how to properly use a nasal aspirator on a baby. And that lesson has come in handy with seven grandkids.

Seeking God for Resources

God also assured me as I began to seek him with my worries that he would teach me everything I needed to know to care for my firstborn.

As an eighteen-year-old mom, I had no skills to care for my child. Even though I had two younger sisters, I felt totally ill prepared to take care of my own son. I knew I would make terrible mistakes, and I thought he deserved a much more experienced and intelligent mother. And I battled depression for a long time.

I feared caring for the needs of my son—I wanted what was best for him. Yet I sensed God gave me the assurance that he chose me to be Adam's mom.

Remember, God had already convinced me that he had a plan and a purpose for both of our lives. And he had taught me that he would cover my mistakes.

I also learned that God never calls us to do something without providing the resources we need to do it.

In Philippians 1, Paul and Timothy encourage the believers at Philippi with a promise: "And I am certain that God, who began the good work within you, will continue his work until it is finally finished" (Phil. 1:6 NLT).

I know that God has a plan for my life now, too. And part of his plan is sharing many of the life lessons I've learned about the power of his Word with others. Every day, I still sense an urgency to seek God, even when no problems threaten my well-being.

Not too long ago, Adam celebrated his fortieth birthday. And I could not help but remember the promise God gave me about him a few days after his birth. "Not a single one of all the good promises the LORD had given to [our] family . . . was left unful-filled; everything he had spoken came true" (Joshua 21:45 NLT).

My role as a mother has evolved over the years, and I still have my doubts at times about my ability to meet the needs of my extended family. But I must confess that God has been faithful to keep his promises, even when I couldn't seem to keep mine.

Looking for Jesus

Thinking he was in their company, they traveled on for a day. Then they began looking for him among their relatives and friends. When they did not find him, they went back to Jerusalem to look for him. (Luke 2:44–45 NIV)

Have you ever lost your child? Then you can imagine the panic that Mary and Joseph experienced when they realized their twelve-year-old son was missing.

Although I never lost either of my children for days, I can remember the utter panic I felt when my daughter, Tara, was lost in the woods for a few hours with a friend. My imagination and fear consumed my thoughts. *Has she been kidnapped? Has she fallen into the lake nearby?*

When we finally found her, I probably responded like Mary: "[Why] have you done this to us? Your father and I have been half out of our minds looking for you" (Luke 2:48 *The Message*).

I've also experienced the grief of waiting for my prodigal child to come home and losing hope when she continued to drift away from us.

In my desperate search, I prayed, *"Jesus, where are you? You promised to stay right here with us!"* I wondered why he didn't just "show up" and answer our prayers right away.

Sometimes I'm tempted to give up on faith when Jesus doesn't fulfill his promises to me as I imagined he would. I believe he is my healer, my deliverer, my victory, and my provider. Yet I still don't always see him answer my prayers as I expect.

When I've faced impossible situations where God didn't respond as I wanted, I've been reminded of who I am (his child) and who he is (my Savior). And I return to him broken and empty, begging for mercy and understanding.

I've wondered about the scene with Jesus, after his parents found him in the temple. Earlier, I had assumed this scenario just revealed a little of Jesus's humanity as a child. But the story takes on a new meaning when I realize that Jesus is not always where I expect him to be either, especially during a crisis:

> Thinking he was in their company, they traveled on for
> a day. Then they began looking for him among their
> relatives and friends. When they did not find him,
> they went back to Jerusalem to look for him. After
> three days they found him in the temple courts, sitting
> among the teachers, listening to them and asking them
> questions . . . When his parents saw him, they were
> astonished. His mother said to him, "Son, why have you
> treated us like this? Your father and I have been anx-
> iously searching for you." (Luke 2:44–48 NIV)

I can imagine the panic Jesus's mother felt after searching for him for three days. Can't you? Any parent who has lost her child while shopping can relate to her reaction.

When I read this story, I pictured Jesus responding to his mom like my grandson Miles did to me after he disappeared in a clothing store.

My heart skipped a beat when I realized he was gone. I started yelling for him, frantically asking everyone if they had seen him. I was about to call the mall security when I saw his little shoes sticking out from under the ladies' dresses. After I hugged his neck, I scolded him for hiding from me.

Miles responded to my panic with an innocent smile: "I just wanted to sit down, Nonnie. I'm tired of shopping."

How could I scold him? He's just related to his "Pop"—my husband Dan, who tries to avoid shopping in the ladies' department of the clothing store, too.

But I don't think Jesus meant to upset or play a trick on his parents. He seemed to be focused on listening and obeying his heavenly Father. And he expected his earthly parents to know where he was—in his Father's house. "But they did not understand what he was saying to them" (Luke 2:50 NIV).

As I prayed about how to apply this scripture to my life, I realized that I'm a lot like Jesus's parents at times. I just assume Jesus is "with me," in the sense that he is pleased with the direction I'm going. Then when I lose my peace and finally begin to seek him, I often find he's at work somewhere else.

What does that look like with me? Sometimes in my "righteous anger" I lose my temper. Then I wonder why I'm convicted about the words that came out of my mouth. After all, "they" were wrong. Right?

Maybe this passage from Ephesians will shed some light on that subject for us:

> Do not let any unwholesome talk come out of your
> mouths, but only what is helpful for building others up
> according to their needs, that it may benefit those who
> listen. And do not grieve the Holy Spirit of God, with
> whom you were sealed for the day of redemption. Get
> rid of all bitterness, rage and anger, brawling and
> slander, along with every form of malice. Be kind and
> compassionate to one another, forgiving each other, just
> as in Christ God forgave you. (Eph. 4:29–32 NIV)

If I'm convicted about my words, maybe I spoke when I should've been quiet. Were the words I used "helpful for building others up according to their need"? Or were they full of "bitterness, rage and anger, brawling and slander"?

God's Word assures me that I always find him if I diligently seek him: "You will seek me and find me when you seek me with all your heart" (Jer. 29:13 NIV).

Even if I look up and it seems like Jesus has left the room, my red flag emotional response can remind me to stop and seek him, not panic. I can be sure that God is just getting my attention. And he wants me to stop and surrender my emotions and the situation to him.

I'm grateful I can trust him to work behind the scenes. Aren't you? Remember, you just might find him "in the temple," or in that intensive-care waiting room, "sitting in the midst of the doctors, both hearing them, and asking them questions" (Luke 2:46 KJV).

This truth has comforted me in some of my waiting rooms, wondering why my prayers for healing or deliverance weren't answered for my loved ones in the way I had hoped.

Red Flags of Worry Guide Me as I Seek God

Mother's death arrived after an intense time of caregiving I shared with my siblings, and it preceded another season of caregiving with my daughter, Tara.

Tara was unable to attend Mother's funeral due to her pregnancy. When we returned to Arkansas a few days later, I didn't even have time to unpack. As I arrived in Little Rock, I had to go with Tara to the hospital.

This forced me to move back into full-time caregiving again, supporting my daughter through childbirth and recovery, because she needed help with her two other children.

Life became even more challenging during the next few years. Tara faced three serious surgeries, and her family continued to grow, adding two more children. My daughter-in-law Jenni also experienced major health crises with several miscarriages and two difficult pregnancies. Then a routine, low-risk surgery developed into a terminal illness for my father-in-law. So I spent many weeks of the next eighteen months in Texas helping my mother-in-law, Mary, care for him.

I mention these trials to illustrate a few of the ongoing family issues I faced for seven years following Mother's death. At the time, I knew my worrisome circumstances were causing many stress-related health problems for me. I couldn't eat properly. I couldn't sleep. I couldn't concentrate on my work. I couldn't talk about anything without becoming emotionally distressed during the conversation. And my anxiety level increased each day.

I tried to pray about my worries, but I just couldn't find the words to say. But still, the Holy Spirit continued to remind me of the spiritual insights I'd already learned.

Mother's illness and death led me to a place I'd never been with my emotions. I faced mental anguish and terrible emotional battles I could not win every day. And through it all, God reminded me of the spiritual victories of my past days—how he has always been with me and how he pursued me even during the difficult circumstances of my life when I did not seek him.

I would prefer to say that I've always sought God in my life, but that would not be true. In fact, God has drawn me near even when I failed to seek him first. But through all the difficulties in my life, I can look back and see evidence of God seeking my attention.

The Lord used red flags of worry to teach me to rely on him. And even when I wasn't responsive, he continued to pursue me, especially when my circumstances grew more difficult.

Thus far along our journey, I've shared my response to God during my crisis of faith, but I haven't told you about the times that I turned away from him, refusing to obey his leadership.

I ignored his guidance when he was leading me to resign from my job. Because of my stubbornness, I stayed, and the job continued to get more difficult, not easier. But there were other times I did obey and my circumstances still grew more difficult.

I understand why someone who might be aware of our history might question the decision to follow Jesus. It's not an easy road. Hebrews 12:7–11 says God disciplines us and prunes away the fruitless branches of our lives:

> Endure hardship as discipline; God is treating you as his children. For what children are not disciplined by their father? If you are not disciplined—and everyone undergoes discipline—then you are not legitimate, not true sons and daughters at all. Moreover, we have all had human fathers who disciplined us and we respected them for it. How much more should we submit to the Father of spirits and live! They disciplined us for a little while as they thought best; but God disciplines us for our good, in order that we may share in his holiness. No discipline seems pleasant at the time, but painful. Later on, however, it produces a harvest of righteousness and peace for those who have been trained by it. (NIV)

Seeking God in Hard Times

Are you overwhelmed by stress in your life? What helps you handle those times?

The book of Lamentations offers a clear word on how to deal with difficult days: "When life is heavy and hard to take, go off by yourself. Enter the silence. Bow in prayer. Don't ask questions: Wait for hope to appear" (Lam. 3:28–29 *The Message*).

As I studied the words of this scripture, I discovered five spiritual strategies that have helped me as I chose to seek God during the difficult seasons of life—solitude, silence, prayer, listening, and waiting. The chapters that follow discuss these five helpful approaches, starting with the first strategy, solitude.

Solitude

Spending Time Alone

[G]o off by yourself . . . (Lam. 3:28–29 The Message*)*

As the sun rises over the red clay tile roofs of Salamanca, Spain, I gaze in awe at the horizon of a country and culture unique and diverse from my own home. I can't believe I've been given the opportunity to study abroad with some other students from Arkansas.

I walk away from the balcony of my rented room to face my Spanish experience, and I unlock the bedroom door of my temporary housing with caution. I hear dishes clinking in the kitchen and my stomach rumbles, smelling bread toasting and strong coffee brewing. But I ease down the long, narrow hall, hesitant to greet my new Spanish host family.

I peek around the framed door opening into the kitchen, and Beni, my exchange student hostess, welcomes me with a smile.

When she offers me café con leche and pan tostado, I acknowledge her kindness. But when I sit down in the padded metal chair of her 1950s-style kitchen table, I encounter more differences than commonalities.

Beni only speaks Spanish, and I struggle to understand her unique accent. When I attempt to communicate in her language, she wrinkles her brow with confusion. We both stumble through our first of many conversations and meals together this summer.

Beni offers to guide me across town to the Spanish language school, a half-hour walk. So I rush to my room, grab my backpack, and pray, *Lord, help me remember everything I need.*

I notice my map, folded neatly on my bed, and tuck it into one of the outside pockets of my bag. As I tiptoe to the exit, the tile floor creaks and a groan erupts from a bedroom where Beni's two adult sons sleep.

Do they perceive me as an intruder in their home? The front door sticks as I try to open it. Then I step toward Beni, who is waiting for me at the elevator. The door slams shut behind me, echoing in the empty hallway. I cringe again—silence seems impossible.

Eight floors down, "la Avenida Federica Anaya" awaits us.

The morning walk with Beni invites me into the daily rituals of Salamanca. The merchants prepare for their customers—students, tourists, and locals. The sidewalks glisten as the shopkeepers dowse the stone pavement with mops and buckets of soapy water. A delivery boy quickly steps to one side to avoid a careless splash. An older gentleman struggles with a long, slender pole cranking up the gate covering the door and large window of his shop. A young, lanky assistant waits to raise the tattered, maroon canopy that shades the entrance from the brilliant morning sunlight.

A pungent odor surprises me as I pass the meat market, quickly displaced by the aroma of freshly baked bread from the corner bakery just ahead. Across the way, a strange rattle calls my attention to the paperboy's rickety cart. One middle-aged lady glances at the headlines as she sits on a wrought-iron bench bolted to the sidewalk. The streets fill with chattering people, hustling to work and school.

Most Spanish natives and tourists walk wherever they go, although occasional buses and worn-out taxis pick up the crosstown commuters. Very few residents own cars or motorcycles—walkers outnumber motorists ten to one. Some neighbors stroll with their dogs on the narrow patches of grass between the sidewalks and the streets; the canine visitations keep the grass green and healthy.

The young people dress in a faddish mode, but the older residents don more old-fashioned, somewhat formal, styles. Very rarely do residents wear sneakers with their everyday apparel; they save athletic shoes for their sports attire. Colorful, immodest shorts and white Nikes identify the foreign tourists.

As I arrive at la Escuela Internacional, Beni slips away and I greet my travel companions from Arkansas. Although a generation gap separates us, I exchange stories with my foreign travel companions like a "normal" college student. We plan to meet later that evening to muster moral support.

I struggle with the first few classes because the instructors—also a decade or more younger than me—insist that we speak Spanish only. They constantly rebuke students who forget their strict language rules. But during our break between classes, I hear students conversing in several dialects—French, German, English, and a few unfamiliar tongues.

After classes, I walk back to Beni's home with a friend, arriving twenty minutes late for the midday meal. My hosts retreat from the table, ignoring me, obviously offended by my tardiness. Silence replaces all conversations, including my introduction to the rest of the family. A prepared plate awaits me on their kitchen table, so I eat alone as punishment.

The people of Spain boast of their Mediterranean-style cuisine. Typical meals include seafood, hard-crusted bread, fresh vegetables, fruit, and olive oil. Many American students despise Spain's meal schedule. They complain of hunger as they wait for the delayed midafternoon lunch. But visitors enjoy the long siesta that follows. Even the merchants close their shops for a midday break. I decide to take advantage of the rest period. So I retreat to my bedroom, where I write in my journal and prepare homework— several lengthy assignments due the next day.

Around 5:00 PM, the town reawakens and resumes its busy schedule. I abandon my temporary refuge to attend the new student orientation. To ensure my prompt arrival, I allow myself two hours to walk to the school while exploring the city. As I pick up the apartment keys left on my desk by Beni, I try to recall my previous guided path through the streets of Salamanca from the morning walk.

As I attempt to find my way to the Plaza Mayor, my internal compass fails me. The streets of Salamanca spoke around the Plaza Mayor, their cultural center, like spokes on a wagon wheel. And as I wander the maze of this romantic city, I lose my way, unable to read the fine print on my city map because of the quickly fading sunset. Fearful thoughts inch their way into my mind, and panic threatens my confidence.

When I ask for directions, I cannot find the right Spanish words to voice my questions. I approach a man standing outside his gift shop and attempt to ask him for directions. Without speaking, he points to the local tourist shop down the block. My lack of language and directional skills annoy the lady in the visitor center—I suppose she had already answered too many inquiries. Finally, an observant onlooker offers his assistance, but I fear ulterior motives in his congenial nature. So I excuse myself, rushing away even more confused and frustrated.

A cloud of doubt and worry trails me. I consider calling Beni for help. *Will she understand my request? What about my Arkansas friends? How can I reach them? Will they wonder why I missed the orientation? Will they look for me?*

Frantic and afraid, I ease down on the stone curb. On the verge of tears, I place my face in my hands. Then I draw another deep breath and offer a desperate plea, "Jesus . . . help me!"

My despair, expressed in those simple words, leaves me feeling empty and weak. As I look up, I search for some familiar landmark.

To my surprise, I notice a street sign illuminated in the shadows—la calle de Jesús.

Jesus Street! I exhale in relief and smile, *Thank You, Jesus!*

A familiar scripture comes to mind: "Have I not commanded you? Be strong and courageous. Do not be afraid; do not be discouraged, for the LORD your God will be with you wherever you go" (Josh. 1:9 NIV).

I gather my belongings and stand up, feeling my strength returning after my emotional meltdown. And as I walk the few blocks back to the Plaza, I catch a glimpse of the golden arches of the American restaurant where I had agreed to meet my friends.

Later, as I detail my traumatic experience to my unbelieving, scholarly friends, they laugh at my "spiritual" epiphany. But I know—without a doubt—that a greater power watches over my journey always. And once again, I sensed his peace and protection, guiding my exploration of Salamanca.

Jesus Street Reflection

My journey as a writer often challenges me to take risks and venture alone into unfamiliar territory. From the academic world to the Christian publishing marketplace, my explorations carry me beyond the borders of my Arkansas home.

I confessed my desperation to the Lord when I was lost in Spain and God led me to "Jesus Street." But I still had to face five more weeks in Salamanca, struggling with my inept language skills, aging body, and poor eyesight.

Yet when I remembered that the Lord was always with me, I did not feel so alone and helpless. And day after day, he gave me the resources and strength I needed to complete the semester and return to Arkansas, knowing his presence would always be with me.

Times of Preparation and Testing

Jesus knew the importance of spending time alone with his Father. When he needed to listen, he would pull away from everyone else.

Prior to the most important moments of his life, Jesus would seek a solitary place to listen to his Father. After he miraculously fed five thousand people, "he climbed the mountain so he could be by himself and pray. He stayed there alone, late into the night" (Matt. 14:23 *The Message*).

This time of solitude for Jesus proved to be a time of testing. But notice how Jesus responded earlier to his tempter:

Next Jesus was taken into the wild by the Spirit for the Test. The Devil was ready to give it. Jesus prepared for the Test by fasting forty days and forty nights. That left him, of course, in a state of extreme hunger, which the Devil took advantage of in the first test: "Since you are God's Son, speak the word that will turn these stones into loaves of bread."

Jesus answered by quoting Deuteronomy: "It takes more than bread to stay alive. It takes a steady stream of words from God's mouth."

For the second test the Devil took him to the Holy City. He sat him on top of the Temple and said, "Since you are God's Son, jump." The Devil goaded him by quoting Psalm 91: "He has placed you in the care of angels. They will catch you so that you won't so much as stub your toe on a stone."

Jesus countered with another citation from Deuteronomy: "Don't you dare test the Lord your God."

For the third test, the Devil took him to the peak
of a huge mountain. He gestured expansively, pointing
out all the earth's kingdoms, how glorious they all were.
Then he said, "They're yours—lock, stock, and barrel.
Just go down on your knees and worship me, and they're
yours."

Jesus' refusal was curt: "Beat it, Satan!" He backed
his rebuke with a third quotation from Deuteronomy:
"Worship the Lord your God, and only him. Serve him
with absolute single-heartedness."

The Test was over. The Devil left. And in his place,
angels! Angels came and took care of Jesus' needs. (Matt.
4:1–11 *The Message*)

We see Jesus searching for solitude both before his ministry began
and shortly before his crucifixion. Both were difficult times, but
they were also when he was accepting the most challenging assignments of his life. And during these times, Jesus teaches us how to
face our temptations—with the Word of God.

Letting Go

I've had moments like that—when I had to let go of every other
responsibility, step out in faith into the next challenge, and face
another time of testing.

One critical period was when I got married. I left behind one
season of my life to accept the next. And I had to let go of some
things that made me feel secure. But new challenges and seasons
of life demand that we release one thing in order to grasp the next.

That happened once again when Dan and I moved our family
from our hometown to attend seminary. We had to walk away from

loved ones, jobs, friends, a new house, and countless other things to go forward and follow Christ.

Now I'm in that place again. I sense a need to let go of some things with my husband's retirement. I need to abandon some things I've been doing and rethink my future commitments for us to be able to make new plans and enjoy this new season of our lives. And I know resisting change will be painful until I finally let go of my own plans and allow God to lead us both in the coming days.

It's odd how the Holy Spirit guides us. I've known for a long time that he guides us with his peace. But I don't always recognize his guidance when it comes. So when I lose that sense of peace, I know the red flag is waving for me to seek God again until I find God's peace.

Often it helps to go to a solitary place where I can hear from the Lord in the quiet. This doesn't always require a change of location. It could involve a change of mind-set—where I am forced to let go of the past and move forward.

At times, these changes come for me in a family change or crisis—like a birth, marriage, illness, death, new job, or move. I can remember many days when I had to be alone with God to ask for his guidance.

Sometimes I've consulted others for their advice or opinion. But I find this to be a waste of time and effort if I'm resisting God's direction. For instance, if I compare myself to other writers, it is counterproductive. Even though there are common denominators, we are not the same.

This is true in other areas of life. Not everyone chooses the same paths. At times, I get caught up being too concerned over what others think about what I'm doing. When I do, my focus wanders because I am listening to people rather than God.

The Lord encourages me to embrace change. And in the process I need to dismiss some things in order to be able to follow him. I'm choosing to trust him to show me what to do, and he promises to give me the strength to do it. And "I know whom I have believed, and am convinced that he is able to guard what I have entrusted to him until that day" (2 Tim. 1:12 NIV).

Defining Solitude

What does *solitude* mean to you?

My online dictionary defines it as "the state or situation of being alone." But it also refers to a state of mind—where we refocus our thoughts, escaping from the distractions and worries that surround us.

Although I spend quite a bit of time alone in my empty nest, finding mental solitude can still feel impossible at times.

If you're a stay-at-home mom, chasing kids around the house all day, you may long for solitude. You may look forward to the time when your little birds have abandoned the nest.

Do you dream of the day when you can sit down, read a good book, and drink a cup of java without a toddler jumping up in your lap, knocking your book to the floor, and spilling your hot coffee?

I recall those long and lonely days as a young mom when I longed for some adult conversation. And I thanked the Lord for providing our church's weekly Mothers' Day Out program.

Struggle with Solitude

I've always needed a healthy balance of human interaction and solitude.

My son Adam still laughs about the times when I would lock myself in the bathroom for a good cry. He doesn't joke about that memory as much now, since he's married with children of his own.

Now that my kids have homes of their own, I can usually find a more comfortable place of solitude, better than my bathroom. Instead of struggling to find a way to retreat from a busy household, the challenge is learning how to silence my phone and disconnect from social media.

My writing life requires periods of time without distraction. Then, at other times, the silence itself becomes my distraction. I still struggle with the solitude that this season demands.

Yes, I still need my space—like my grandchildren, who crave "alone time" to escape from constant sibling companionship. At other times, I become restless in the isolation, longing for human connection.

I've found that walking the wooded trails near my home reenergizes me. Often, I take my lawn chair, computer, and camera to the lakefront to work, or I take a short drive and visit a coffee shop to refresh my mood.

My most creative writing ideas come when I'm alone, outside my writing cave. I observe a beautiful sunrise. Or I watch a doe with her young fawn grazing in the woods behind my backyard.

In the solitude, God speaks to me through his written Word. But often he speaks to me through the beauty of his creation. As I meditate on the sights and sounds around me, I find evidence of his love everywhere I go.

Silence

Tuning Out Distractions

Enter the silence. (Lam. 3:28 The Message)

I paused in the doorway to Tara's former bedroom, staring at the walls in desperate need of a fresh coat of paint. An empty bulletin board was securely nailed to one wall, and a few colored thumbtacks remained as evidence of her high school photos and posters. Loud music no longer rattled the windows in this barren room—unbearable silence replaced it. Both of my fledglings had abandoned our nest, and our home seemed parched and stodgy.

What could I do to fill the void and replace my exaggerated imaginations of the past? I needed a fresh vision for my life.

Children filled our home with activity and sounds of excitement and drama throughout my adult life. Our firstborn, Adam, arrived a few weeks before our first wedding anniversary. But he quickly grew up and moved out, soon followed by his younger sister, Tara.

I recall the pine bunk beds that once lined the wall behind me. Recently, we shuttled them to an apartment across town. A homemade wooden toy chest in our garage now stored the thrillers and scary mysteries from Tara's bookcase. Clothes hangers dangled in the closet like cheap wind chimes as reminders of prom dresses and letterman jackets.

Dan tried to encourage me by replacing my upright circa 1950 piano with a trendy keyboard. By positioning it near the window, I could enjoy my jonquils, dogwood blossoms, and azaleas while I made music.

We had baptized our flower beds with tears during a crisis with our teenage daughter. Gardening had been my most effective way of escaping my humiliation and pain.

Perhaps I could watch my favorite movies while I worked on my craft projects if I reclaimed our old television and video player for the room. I could use Tara's abandoned stereo unit, long since displaced by a compact disc player.

Even the prospects of music and flowers didn't smooth out the wrinkles in my brow. But I couldn't pinpoint the root of my emotional discomfort. *Why not buy new bedroom furniture and forget it?* My unsettled feelings frustrated me. *Why all the confusion over how to revitalize this room?*

As I reflected on the vacant room, questions about my journey emerged. I felt vacant and abandoned, just as the room appeared. I had heard horror stories about the "empty nest syndrome." I had reasoned, *This will never be a problem for me. By the time my kids leave our nest, I'll be the one ready to fly.* But as I celebrated completing my task of shaping the next generation's character, I found myself depressed and lonely. I felt like I had lost my purpose in life, as my role as a mom changed.

My friend Debbie commented one day, "You've finally got the chance to do anything you want. What are you going to do now?"

Then a question that Adam asked me many years ago surfaced, "What are you going to be when you grow up, Mom?"

Adam attended elementary school at the time. He expected everyone, even a stay-at-home mom, to eventually go to work. His penetrating insight nagged me over the years. Now I faced his question again. *What was I going to be, now that I'd "grown up"?* As new thoughts of my future flirted with my daydreams, my lack of purpose haunted me.

I confessed my emptiness and frustration to the Lord. I recalled his words to Joshua as he grieved the loss of his beloved Moses. As the Lord prepared him to enter his promised land, he instructed Joshua to meditate on his Word. God also promised Joshua, "I will never leave you nor forsake you" (Josh. 1:5 NIV).

My own passion for God's Word and for writing about my faith had led me to enroll in a writing class during my seminary years. One of my first essays was even published in a denominational periodical. I wondered, *Could God actually be calling me to write?*

I knew that I would need professional training to be taken seriously as a writer. But would it be possible to go back to college? Could our budget handle the tuition and debt? As I considered my unresolved questions, answers and hope emerged. *What would it feel like to walk on a university campus again?*

Another scripture encouraged me: "Be strong and courageous. Do not be afraid; do not be discouraged, for the Lord your God will be with you wherever you go" (Josh. 1:9 NIV).

As I redecorated our bedrooms, I painted the walls eggshell white to help breathe life back into those musty spaces, transforming the area into a spacious study chamber. It would be the perfect setting for my computer, where I could read and write without interruptions. I added a comfortable chair and a brass floor lamp for reading. The varnished oak bookcase my dad built many years ago fit nicely on one wall.

New life appeared, and I welcomed it like the daffodils breaking through the soil of the flowerbed after the long, cold winter. Although I sensed great change, I became resolute in my mission. While the threat of having to accept the solitude of my house made one last attempt to drown me with self-pity, I decided to embrace this new way of thinking and living.

As I settled into my new office, the promises of the future lifted me like an incoming tide. And I knew "with all [my] heart and soul that not one of all the good promises the LORD [my] God gave [me had] failed. Every promise [had] been fulfilled; not one [had] failed" (Josh. 23:14 NIV).

White Space

Therefore do not worry about tomorrow, for tomorrow will worry about itself. Each day has enough trouble of its own. (Matt. 6:34 NIV)

Where do I begin? Do I work on one of these book proposals? Do I need to write another blog post? Do I have a speaking event scheduled this month? Do I need to work on my website?

I didn't know where to start! And I thought, *Enough!*

At first, I thought my confusion might be a response to the stress. Soon, I realized that I needed God's help. I needed some white space!

As a writer, I know the importance of white space—the empty space in every document, in the margins and between the words, graphs, and pictures.

The wise use of this white space can vastly improve communicating the writer's message. And a lack of white space makes the page seem too busy, cluttered, and difficult to read. Yet too much white space produces an incomplete appearance.

White Space of Life

As I planned my use of time and resources, I concluded that the same important rules apply to the white space in all areas of my life.

If I fill every minute of the day with activities, work, and conversation, I become too preoccupied with unproductive distractions. But too much inactivity can rob me of my self-worth and credibility.

How do we determine the amount of white space in our lives? Never underestimate the power of organization, calendars, and spring-cleaning!

Can we discern how much white space to build into our lives? Those who know us best and love us unconditionally can offer healthy opinions. But seek an advisor with extreme caution—you may need to endure unsolicited criticism.

White Space of Grace

Never underestimate the power of God's Word as you manage the white space in your schedule and decisions.

Jesus promised, "I have much more to say to you, more than you can now bear. But when he, the Spirit of truth, comes, he will guide you into all the truth. He will not speak on his own; he will speak only what he hears, and he will tell you what is yet to come" (John 16:12–13 NIV).

As I prayed for direction, I remembered other encouraging words: "Whatever you have learned or received or heard from me, or seen in me—put it into practice. And the God of peace will be with you" (Phil. 4:9 NIV).

I also recalled the story in the Bible of another weak, tormented soul who discovered the sufficiency of God's grace. Like me, the apostle Paul begged God to take away his problems. But God responded with surprising direction: "My grace is enough; it's all you need. My strength comes into its own in your weakness" (2 Cor. 12:9 *The Message*).

The Bible offers important advice about letting go and moving forward:

> Not that I have already obtained all this, or have already arrived at my goal, but I press on to take hold of that for which Christ Jesus took hold of me. Brothers and sisters, I do not consider myself yet to have taken hold of it. But one thing I do: Forgetting what is behind and straining toward what is ahead, I press on toward the goal to win the prize for which God has called me heavenward in Christ Jesus. (Phil. 3:12–14 NIV)

Watch Your Words

Fathers [and Mothers], don't exasperate your children by coming down hard on them. Take them by the hand and lead them in the way of the Master. (Eph. 6:4 The Message)

I glanced up the hill behind our home and had eye contact with a doe as she hovered over her fawn. As I watered my potted tomato plants on my wooden deck, the doe stepped closer to check my reaction to her movements. I remained painfully still, knowing that a sudden movement would cause them to bolt away in fear.

A few minutes later, as I adjusted my hose, I saw the doe walking quietly away from me, grazing on the grass and plucking leaves from the low-hanging branches.

Without any words, I understood this message from nature, loud and clear: "We feel safe here if you don't make any sudden moves that threaten us."

As I observed the doe and her spotted fawn, I thought of my daughter, Tara, and her five children: *How many times have I unintentionally shooed away my children with my impulsive words or quick temper?* Too many to count.

The deer's caution exposed a warning about approaching those that I love. First, do no harm!

Am I cautious with my movements and reactions as I interact with my children and grandchildren? I'm rethinking that question now.

In one instance, after I expressed my concerns and expectations to my daughter about one of her children, I regretted my hasty words and unsolicited advice. So I offered a heartfelt apology, hoping for her forgiveness. I realized that words often bring unintended consequences and are not always readily welcomed nor appreciated.

Sometimes our silence is more effective than our words. I know my voice can frighten an animal or bird, but sometimes I forget that a harsh word or angry tone of voice can also repel a child, friend, or other loved one.

We employ our written and spoken words to convey our thoughts and feelings. But at times, we fail to guard our choice of words, refusing to consider their impact on others. As a writer, I know I need to revise my work. But I ignore the importance of editing my words when I fail to "be quick to listen, slow to speak, and slow to get angry" (James 1:19 NLT). And I undermine my influence.

When the doe appeared in my backyard again, I knew to be calm and quiet. Opening a squeaky door or stepping on dry, parched leaves would send her scampering with her fawn close behind.

As I watched the deer quietly steal away a few minutes later, I thanked God for the lessons he provides for me in nature for my own family and for my writing life. I offered a prayer of thanksgiving for sharing in his truth, expressed in nature and in everyday life. Then I asked him to help me release my children and give up my selfish expectations once again.

What opinions and expectations will you consider releasing to the Lord?

Stressed Out

Before Hurricane Ike destroyed the Bolivar Peninsula and city of Galveston on the Texas Gulf Coast, another powerful storm landed there a few years earlier—Hurricane Rita. My sister Cathy and her husband Richard lived in Crystal Beach at the time.

After Hurricane Rita passed, Cathy called to give me an update on their situation. And she told me an interesting story about her neighbor's cat.

Cathy's neighbor, Belinda, adopted a stray cat and named him Whisper. Later, she decided to get Whisper neutered and declawed. But after his extreme makeover, Belinda's house was engulfed by fire with Whisper trapped inside. After the smoke cleared, Whisper had vanished. And Belinda moved to her son's home nearby while her home was being rebuilt.

Soon after the fire, Hurricane Rita visited the same area, and Belinda's family was forced to evacuate. So if Whisper ever did return, he would need to fend for himself.

After the storm, Belinda returned to her son's home, and she still couldn't find her cat. Days later, she spotted her dazed and confused pet wandering around their property.

But Whisper had changed. When Belinda offered him food, he resisted. In fact, Whisper kept his distance from everyone.

"I can't imagine what's wrong with him!" Belinda confessed to Cathy and Richard.

"You can't?" Richard responded. "In the past few weeks, he's been 'fixed,' declawed, caught in a house fire, tossed around by a hurricane, and abandoned with no food. I can't imagine what's wrong with him either!"

As I listened to Cathy's story about Whisper, I knew Cathy and Richard had also faced stressful circumstances caused by the storm damage. As Rita approached the coast, they were forced to pack all their valuables and evacuate to their daughter's home in Arkansas—with their children, grandchildren, and in-laws.

After the storm, Cathy grieved over their losses. No one had electricity on the peninsula for weeks. They had to remove debris around their home. And Richard had to clear the fallen trees around his elderly parents' home. Since their home and beach property had been damaged, they also had to wait on insurance adjusters before they could proceed with the repairs.

As Cathy talked about all the devastation to the area, she mentioned the destruction of all the cedar trees in our family's cemetery. It had only been a few months since we'd buried our mother there, next to our dad. The past few weeks had traumatized Cathy.

Cathy admitted her depressed feelings as we talked. "I can't understand why I can't get back into the swing of things!"

"You can't?" I responded. "Maybe you're all feeling a little bit like Whisper. In the past few weeks, you've been forced to evacuate your home, to live with distant relatives for several weeks, and to clear fallen trees and debris. Now you're waiting on an insurance company to discuss repairing the damages to your home. I'd imagine anybody might be feeling a little stressed out!"

Silence and Prayer

Where do we run when we're pursued by our own fears and worries?

I'm often distracted by worries and responsibilities while I'm trying to get a handle on my emotions. I've learned that I must choose to tune out everything that prevents me from giving full attention to the things that matter most. So I turn off the phone, ignore all other interruptions, and go to the Lord in prayer.

Silence and solitude provide the white space of grace I need to seek God in prayer, and I can listen for his guidance and wait for his hope and peace to return.

Prayer

Communicating with God

Bow in prayer . . . (Lam. 3:29 The Message*)*

I stared from my upstairs window at the autumn leaves as tears ran down my cheeks, drowning in my private sorrow. The cool wind rustled the tops of the oak trees, but inside my home, I could barely breathe. Fear seized my heart and controlled my thoughts.

A squirrel scampered freely across the yard, burying acorns for the coming winter season. But I felt trapped by my new environment, hidden from everyone I knew.

We wanted to move again the week following unloading our furniture into our new home. *How could we have slipped from ecstasy to despair in just a few days? Why did everything seem wrong now that had been so right earlier?*

The move from Texas to Arkansas excited my whole family. Although we struggled when we said farewell to close friends, we anticipated a new chapter unfolding in our family's journey. But within days of our arrival, our circumstances crushed our confidence to rubble.

As I prepared our evening meal after a long, frustrating day, Dan came home from his first day at the new job and announced, "I think I've made a terrible mistake!"

I turned the burner down on the stove so our dinner would simmer, and I quickly walked into the dining room, where he sat with his face in his hands. I put my hand on his shoulder, hoping to console him. We had walked through other crises together, and the reality of our present situation forced both of us to our knees.

Dan's discouragement concerned me because he had been so certain about moving to this new job. Before coming to Arkansas, Dan had anticipated God would move us to a new place of service. We had even discussed the possibilities and prayed for God to guide us and show us exactly where he wanted us to serve him. We were both committed to going wherever we sensed the Lord leading us.

As we prayed, Dan said the name of a city that came to his mind. Still cautious about hearing from God in this way, we agreed to trust God to confirm his direction for us.

Dan anticipated the move for weeks, praying God would either move us or relieve his restlessness. With no clear answer revealed, Dan reconciled that the stress of his job had possibly led him to conjure up his intense desire to move, because no job opportunity surfaced in the new location. A few months later, after we thought we put the matter to rest, Dan received a surprising call. Someone had recommended him for a position in Little Rock, Arkansas.

"Is that the city that came to mind when we prayed about moving a few months ago?" I asked him.

Dan's face turned pale as he tried to hold back his tears. Speechless, he just shook his head in agreement. Little Rock was the place he sensed God directing us when we prayed earlier. So, within a few weeks, Dan accepted the new job there.

Even though neither of us had ever been to Little Rock, we both had peace that God was confirming his will for us.

As we prepared to move to our new home, I looked forward to the beautiful landscapes and the four distinct seasons in Arkansas. I sensed God had fulfilled this promise to us: "You will go out in joy and be led forth in peace; the mountains and hills will burst into song before you, and all the trees of the field will clap their hands" (Isa. 55:12 NIV).

But as soon as we arrived, we faced the intense heat of the summer. And our circumstances made us begin to doubt God's direction.

As I remembered everything that had happened to prepare us for Arkansas—Dan's restlessness, praying for direction, God speaking "Little Rock," and the confirming call with a job offer—I wondered, *Why all the doubts now?*

Dan had never second-guessed a major decision like this. And I had always been impressed by his determination and decisiveness.

Now in a new city and home, uncertainty hovered over our household throughout our first summer. Friends, schools, coworkers, and even our relationships in our church caused us to regret our decision to move here. The people we met were friendly but seemed so different from us. I wondered, *Will we ever fit in?*

The following days and weeks proved Dan's first reactions to be accurate. He still felt like he was not a good fit at work. And he continued to search for a way of escape, calling former employers and friends about other opportunities.

Chaos visited our household, troubling our souls. Any place seemed better than Arkansas in those months.

Each morning, I found myself engaged in spiritual warfare for my husband—I sensed his desperate need of prayer support. And when he returned home at night, he seemed discouraged and depressed. The man who previously held his position at work had died unexpectedly, and Dan felt overwhelmed with his workload and the lack of resources and information available to him.

As Dan struggled with doubts, I became aware of how God had prepared me to move to Little Rock. He had provided strong, biblical teaching on prayer—especially to wage spiritual warfare—while we lived in Texas. But I never anticipated that I would need to live out my faith so quickly after departing from our spiritual training ground. Plus, I never considered that following God would be so hard, even though the move to seminary from our hometown had tested us just six years earlier.

We also faced disappointments with Adam and Tara's school assignments. The realtor had misinformed us about their schools, and we couldn't move again because of our lease agreement. I cried every morning as I placed Tara, a fifth grader, on a bus to a school in one of the most dangerous neighborhoods in the city, miles from our home. I shivered with fear when I noticed graffiti-like symbols and gang signs on the walls of Adam's new middle school. After taking them to school the first day, I prayed, *Lord, did we miss your guidance moving here? Could this possibly be your will for us?*

Loneliness blurred my vision even more. The high cost of long-distance limited my phone calls back then and further isolated me from my friends and family in Texas.

The fears of the future made me feel helpless—unable to move forward or go back. And I found myself a prisoner in my own home. The situation felt hopeless, and depression limited my hope for the future. I wondered if that long, hot summer would ever end.

As the seasons changed, I continued to battle depression and worry. As a stay-at-home mom, I was alone. We struggled to find a new church, so I had not made many new friends. Dan worked long hours, trying to hang on at work. And Adam and Tara were struggling to adjust to their new schools.

I found I had a lot of time on my hands. Desperate for answers and hope, I spent many hours reading, praying, listening to inspirational music, and studying my Bible. I chose to sit upstairs, near the window, overlooking Indianhead Lake.

When autumn arrived, I found myself captivated by the beautiful fall scenery. The colors glowed in the morning sunlight. The leaves displayed a variety of shades, from crimson to pumpkin, before they turned brown and covered the ground.

The foliage around our home helped soothe my anxious thoughts. But my doubts and fears tormented me. So I questioned God, *Why is this happening to us?*

In the midst of my confusion, I realized, *Those leaves are dying!* I knew their colors would eventually fade, turn brown, and the trees would be barren in a few weeks.

How can death reveal itself in such beauty? As I reflected on the past few weeks, I realized that I felt like I was dying, too.

Then another question came to mind. *Will I ever sense your peace and joy again?* I had grieved over my losses, and I felt exposed like the bare tree branches after shedding their leaves. The cold, frigid days of winter would soon sweep over us. *Even the wild animals know to prepare for season changes. But will we survive until spring?*

Suddenly, a doe appeared in the thicket behind our house. She stood there for a while grazing on a patch of green grass. She could not see me, but her visit comforted me. Although the outside world closed in on her safe pasture, she stood confidently on her turf.

I ran to find my camera—I loved to capture the landscape around our home. Photography proved to be a great escape for me. But before I could focus, the doe faded quickly back into the forest.

Looking out the patio door at the dense brush behind our home, I revisited the events of the past weeks. Then I remembered the promise of spring.

I knew a new season of life would eventually arrive for my family, too. New leaves would bud on our trees, and new friends would sprout like tender plants from the seeds we would sow. This beautiful venue called Arkansas would become our home.

Later that day, I stepped outside to get the mail, and a breeze cooled my face. The summer heat was retreating now. Winter would arrive on schedule in a just few weeks. And I knew this time of discontent would pass.

Peace returned with that fresh autumn wind. Tears of joy now filled my red, swollen eyes. And I found hope as I faced the future with confidence that God would honor our obedience to follow him.

As we shared our story, some friends and family questioned us about hearing from God like we did. Even today, I still find it hard to describe God's voice to someone who has never experienced him. But Jesus answers this question in John 10:27: "My sheep recognize my voice. I know them, and they follow me" (*The Message*).

Now I am aware that God speaks to us all in different ways—he uses whatever means necessary to get our attention. But he will guide us if we ask, even if it means communicating things to us that we might not comprehend at the time.

Since our first summer in Arkansas, three decades ago, God has been faithful to answer when we call on him.

> This is the confidence we have in approaching God: that if we ask anything according to his will, he hears us. And if we know that he hears us—whatever we ask—we know that we have what we asked of him. (1 John 5:14–15 NIV)

Even though God hasn't prevented our difficult circumstances, he's helped us through every crisis. But his answers often come at the last possible moment. So I know that I must never lose hope in him. "Faith is the confidence that what we hope for will actually happen; it gives us assurance about things we cannot see" (Heb. 11:1 NLT).

I've also seen that God does things his way, not mine. In Isaiah, the Lord declares:

"For my thoughts are not your thoughts, neither are
your ways my ways . . . As the heavens are higher than
the earth, so are my ways higher than your ways and my
thoughts than your thoughts." (Isa. 55:8–9 NIV)

If God says he will act, we can trust he will do it:

For no matter how many promises God has made, they
are "Yes" in Christ. And so through him the "Amen" is
spoken by us to the glory of God. (2 Cor. 1:20 NIV)

And when we feel like we're losing our grip and everything looks
hopeless, remember:

He has made everything beautiful in its time. He has also
set eternity in the human heart; yet no one can fathom
what God has done from beginning to end. (Eccles. 3:11
NIV)

God Speaks

*[T]he Word became human and made his home among us. He
was full of unfailing love and faithfulness. And we have seen his
glory, the glory of the Father's one and only Son. (John 1:14 NLT)*

God sent his Word to reveal himself to us.

As I'm thinking of ways to share my understanding of the
power of God's Word, I recall many times God revealed his truth
in my circumstances. It may have been a sunset or a storm. But he
often speaks through scripture or song.

God speaks to us in our everyday life. And when we are troubled, he has provided our natural emotions to warn us to avoid
dangerous unhealthy responses.

How many times have you found yourself worried, and when
you prayed, you were distracted by a phone call, a honking horn,
or a knock at the door?

When I shared words that hinted about the Lord speaking to me to two friends recently, they said that they had never sensed him speaking to them directly.

In that moment, my words seemed inadequate to illustrate how God speaks in ways other than words—through nature, his written Word, or a song. Yet sometimes I hear God's words spoken to me, just as the disciples heard from Jesus in the storm.

God made himself known to the children of Israel with signs and wonders—he led them with a cloud by day and a pillar of fire by night. And he continues to reveal himself today.

In his written Word, he offers us the promise to lead us with his peace. He also gains our attention through our emotions, such as worry and fear. When we lose our peace, the Bible reminds us to seek him.

Yet we often try to figure things out ourselves instead of pausing to recognize God's presence in our lives. Perhaps we forget the promise of the Holy Spirit, who promises to always be with us, no matter what.

Prayer Reflections

When I first understood that prayer is communication with God, I realized it wasn't a scripted monologue. Not only does God want us to confess our needs and our sins to him; he also wants us to profess our faith in him.

One of the first books that I read on prayer was *Prayer: Conversing with God* by Rosalind Rinker.[14] This book introduced me to the concept of talking to God like I speak to a friend. It totally transformed my personal prayer life and praying with others.

As I write about my experience of learning to hear from God, I always remember my first encounter almost four decades ago. God revealed to me how much he loves me.

Since then, I've had many tough issues to overcome. In surviving each one of them, I knew God promised to be with me and to provide all I needed to endure and flourish.

I've always been able to trust the Holy Spirit to speak a "Word" to me when I need it—but I don't always stop and listen until I'm overwhelmed with worry. Yet I've discovered he's always there, waiting for me to seek him, even when I delay.

He desires to speak to you, too. He doesn't want you to feel isolated, facing life alone. He knows your needs, and he knows the answers to all your questions.

You may not understand much about what's going on in your life right now, but he knows your situation. And he wants to walk with you through your most difficult days.

The storms will come and go, whether we trust Jesus or not. But I've found comfort in knowing he's in the boat with me during every storm—even those times I shook my fist in his face because I didn't understand why bad things had happened.

I've begged him to deliver me from several calamities I didn't think I would survive. But I've always made it through every storm. And he was there to heal my wounds and comfort my broken heart when I needed him most.

When I'm confused and overwhelmed by life, the Lord reminds me to seek him first, and he promises to guard my heart and my mind with his peace.

As I sat at my computer today, I prayed for him to give me insights for this book. I felt empty and confused, facing this project with an acute sense of all the other plans and commitments I had made. But, once again, he directed me to REST. And as I found my place of solitude and silence, I bowed my head in prayer, listening and waiting once again for his truth to set me free. He did not fail.

Prayer, Writing, and Healing

Prayer can become as natural as talking with a good friend. Or it can be as intimate as sharing a secret whisper. It can occur any time of day, no matter where you are or what you are doing.

God promises that if we call on his name, he'll listen: "And if we're confident that he's listening, we know that what we've asked for is as good as ours" (1 John 5:15 *The Message*).

Many mornings, I find myself writing to the Lord. For me, writing is the best way for me to communicate. And at times, I don't even know what I want to say until I write it. Writing is a part of my healing process. Somehow I can reveal my heart with a pen and paper.

It doesn't really matter *how* you approach the Lord. He's always ready to listen. And he's faithful to answer. But we must be willing to seek him, wait to hear from him, and then respond in faith.

I pray this chapter rings true for you today. I don't know your circumstances, but the Lord does, and he is waiting for you to ask. He led me to write this just for you today. He knew where you would be today. And he is keenly aware of everything going on in your life.

Whether you are facing life or death, he has been there. And he wants to walk with you through your deepest valleys of despair.

Hearing God

Before I read his book, *Hearing God*,[15] Pastor Peter Lord spoke on this subject to a group of seminary students in Texas, including Dan and I. It was in that chapel service when I first realized that I could hear from God. This thought-provoking concept intrigued me as I considered the possibility that God would speak directly to believers today.

After explaining that God answered prayers in many diverse ways, Pastor Lord challenged his listeners to experiment and see how God might reveal himself. During the concluding five minutes of his presentation, he invited everyone to quietly bow and privately ask God, "How much do you love me?"

Pastor Lord also suggested that each person listen with an open heart and see if God might have a "Word" for them. After a quiet five minutes, he ended the prayer time and asked those who had heard from God or sensed an answer to share their impression.

Some of the students said they heard a song; others had imagined biblical events. A few mentioned that they recalled scripture passages, and others were overcome by strong feelings.

Tears came to Dan's eyes when we exchanged our experiences from the prayer time later.

"I saw blood dropping into the dust in slow motion, and the dust would splash up in response to each drop." He added, "I sensed God saying, 'Look at the blood.'"

Dan explained that he pictured the scene below the cross at the crucifixion of Christ when "one of the soldiers pierced Jesus's side with a spear, bringing a sudden flow of blood and water" (John 19:34 NIV).

Many students and faculty had come to hear from Peter Lord, and the chapel was too small to accommodate the crowd who showed up; students filled the room and spilled over into the hallway. Peter Lord wasn't a scheduled speaker for chapel that day, but he had been asked by a professor to speak with the students about his relationship with God.

At first, I found myself mesmerized by his Jamaican accent, and I was drawn to his conversational preaching style. He focused on the importance of applying biblical truth to our everyday life and developing a meaningful walk with the Lord. He didn't seem to be trying to convince us of anything, and he even shared some of his own personal struggles in his faith.

Peter Lord had challenged us to close our eyes and ask the Lord, *How much do you love me?* Then he encouraged us to just be still and wait to see what the Lord would speak to our hearts.

The impact of that chapel service altered my then shallow understanding about the role of prayer in a believer's life.

Vision of God's Love

As I closed my eyes, I simply asked the Lord, *How much do you love me?*

In my mind's eye, I pictured myself walking on the beach with Jesus. And he was answering all my questions.

That might seem odd to you, and it may not even seem like a valid answer to my question. But I had many doubts at that time in my life, and his response to my prayer was timely and relevant for my future. So when I asked the Lord how much he loved me, he answered me by confirming that he was aware of all my questions and my needs. He was walking right beside me.

I sensed a promise from him that even though I didn't understand all that was taking place in my life, he was aware of every situation. I also accepted his promise that one day he would answer all my questions. The vision of walking on the seashore also indicated to me the Lord understood my need for peace, because the beach has always been a place of escape and freedom for me.

The ocean represents God's promise of how deep and wide his love is for me and also serves as a metaphor of how all my cares will be cast to the bottom of the ocean, never to be retrieved again.

The poem "Footprints in the Sand" reminds me that the Lord is always with me—even when I'm not aware of his presence. Although the authorship of this poem is disputed, I believe this excerpt from Charles Spurgeon's sermon, "The Education of Sons of God," accurately expresses that belief:[16]

> And did you ever walk out upon that lonely desert island upon which you were wrecked and say, "I am alone—alone—ALONE—nobody was ever here before me"? And did you suddenly pull up short as you

noticed, in the sand, the footprints of a man? I remember right well passing through that experience—and when I looked, lo, it was not merely the footprints of a man that I saw, but I thought I knew whose feet had left those imprints. They were the marks of One who had been crucified, for there was the print of the nails. So I thought to myself, "If He has been here, it is no longer a desert island. As His blessed feet once trod this wilderness-way, it blossoms now like the rose and it becomes to my troubled spirit as a very garden of the Lord!"

Psalms 139 offers encouragement as we consider God's unconditional, endless love and his wisdom in knowing how many grains of sand are on the beach:

> *How precious are your thoughts about me, O God.*
> *They cannot be numbered!*
> *I can't even count them;*
> *they outnumber the grains of sand!*
> *And when I wake up,*
> *you are still with me! (Ps. 139:17–18 NLT)*

I've shared my initial experience of hearing God many times to encourage others to listen as they seek God for direction. And, for some, their experience transformed their prayer life, too.

Do you know how much the Lord loves you?

I encourage you pause and ask the Lord this one question, "Lord, how much do you love me?" Then listen for his response and guidance.

> For this is how God loved the world: He gave his one and only Son, so that everyone who believes in him will not perish but have eternal life. God sent his Son into

the world not to judge the world, but to save the world through him. (John 3:16–17 NLT)

Listen

Hearing God

· ·

Don't ask questions . . . (Lam. 3:29 The Message)

I found myself gasping for breath.

One moment I was arguing with a rebellious teenager who had grown steadily distant from me over the years, and the very next breath, I was holding my precious daughter after her heartbreaking confession.

I snuggled up beside Tara and hid with her under the mounds of pillows tossed at the head of her bed. For a moment, I almost felt secure, wrapped up in layers of sheets and blankets. Then I noticed the face of a fierce tiger on the fleece blanket that covered the entire bed, framed by shades of brown. And I sensed fear crouching in the corner, waiting to devour us.

Lord, help me!

I embraced my daughter again. All her resistance was gone as she allowed me to hold her, to cry with her, and to share her pain, sorrow, grief, and fears. No longer was I rejected and ignored like yesterday's fashions. Tara reached for me as if I were the only one on earth she could trust. And I wanted to be that support to my daughter again. I wanted her to need me, not only as her mother but also as her friend and confidant.

It had been years since I had held my daughter in my arms. The little girl I had prayed for, given birth to, tenderly cared for during her childhood maladies, dressed in jeans instead of ruffles, taught to read and write and sing and dance had brushed me aside like eraser dust when puberty ruled her teenage world. I never realized how much I had missed her until this moment of confession.

Then she broke my heart: "Mom, I still sleep with my teddy bear and watch cartoons! How can I ever be a mother?"

How indeed? She was sixteen years old—a high school sophomore. Was she ready? Was I ready?

Tara's next question startled me, "You're not going to make me give up my baby, are you?"

Without hesitation, I replied, "No, we would never make you do that!"

But what would we do? I had a full-time job; we had our son's college tuition to pay. And we were in debt over our heads.

I wanted to run away. But after a lengthy discussion, I calmly suggested, "Why don't you try to get some rest. We'll talk more about this in the morning."

I left Tara's room that night in a state of despair and panic.

As I entered our bedroom, Dan awoke, "What are you doing up so late? We have to work tomorrow."

"Dan . . ." I hesitated.

"What's wrong?" Dan leaned up on one elbow.

"Tara's pregnant!" I barely exhaled the words before I burst into tears again.

Dan bolted out of the bed and came toward me with his arms open wide as if to keep me from falling.

"What?"

But he had heard me. I did not have to repeat my announcement. I could not say it again. He did not want to hear it again, either. I could no longer act like I was under control.

Dan's response to Tara's news surprised us both. He will be the first to admit he has a bad temper at times; but this night, he was calm. At least that's what I saw. He might have been boiling deep down inside, but he showed no signs as he immediately began consoling me.

As Dan took me in his arms, I held him tightly. I could not breathe; my heart felt as if it was going to burst. I held my husband so closely that he probably wondered if I would ever let go.

"What are we going to do, Dan?"

He squeezed me tighter.

I did not want him to let go. I continued to mutter my doubts, "She's just a baby herself, and she's in there crying. I don't know what to do."

Dan spoke as I released him, "You sit down and try to catch your breath. I need to talk to Tara."

"Please don't lose your temper. That's all we need now—for you to lose your temper."

Dan eased into Tara's room. Could he reassure her? I tried to imagine what he would say, but I totally lost control of my emotions again. I could not bear thinking about Dan's tough, fatherly exterior. Would he have compassion on our daughter? Could he? This was not the time for one of his lectures.

I collapsed on our bed, face down, and buried my face in a pillow. Deep convulsing groans rose from within me. I wept so hard that my eyes burned, and I became nauseated

I never found out what exactly Dan said to Tara—at that point, I didn't want to know. Somehow God's grace was sufficient for us that night.

But the next forty-eight hours proved to be more than I could handle. I tried to relax at night while everyone slept, but I could not quit worrying. I knew I needed to get some rest, but I couldn't quit thinking about Tara's situation.

I knew I needed to get back to work after taking a few personal days, but I didn't know how I could face an office full of social workers, counselors, and ministers where we were in the planning stages of a home for unwed mothers. *Perfect timing—how could I possibly hold myself together through one meeting?* I didn't want to talk to anyone—especially religious people.

The night before I was scheduled to return to work, I found myself sobbing as I reflected on Tara's life. And by midnight, my fears caused me to have a full-blown panic attack—I could not stop crying. I sat on the sofa in our family room with my head in my hands, wiping the tears from my face.

Then I lifted my face and heart toward heaven, begging for mercy. *Lord, I just can't fight this battle alone. It's too hard for me!*

I felt empty, like I had just poured out every bit of strength I had left inside of me. *I need you, Lord! We need you, Lord! Help!*

After I prayed, I pictured a scene from a story about the prophet Elisha in 2 Kings 6:15–17, where another servant of God had panicked because of the battle going on around him:

> When the servant of the man of God got up and went out early the next morning, an army with horses and chariots had surrounded the city. "Oh no, my lord! What shall we do?" the servant asked.
>
> "Don't be afraid," the prophet answered. "Those who are with us are more than those who are with them."
>
> And Elisha prayed, "Open his eyes, Lord, so that he may see." Then the Lord opened the servant's eyes, and he looked and saw the hills full of horses and chariots of fire all around Elisha. (2 Kings 6:15–17 NIV)

From that moment on, I sensed God's presence in a supernatural way. By faith, I knew that God was sending his heavenly army to do battle for our family. And somehow things would be all right.

I fell fast asleep. And I experienced a miraculous feeling of peace in realizing the battle would not be ours alone to fight. I knew God was with us to help carry our daughter and our whole family though the difficult days ahead.

As I begged God for mercy, he gave me the first of many promises to hold on to that night: "Do not be afraid or discouraged because of this vast army. For the battle is not yours, but God's" (2 Chron. 20:15 NIV).

Listening

What about listening? Often, my questions interfere with my communication with God—I'm talking instead of listening. But I'm grateful that God is not impatient with me, like I am with others. He's never surprised by my childlike questions or my selfish intentions.

Do you have a difficult time listening? I do. But I've been learning lately about listening, or rather *not* listening. And if I want to hear from God, I must learn to listen for his voice.

As I listen to the songbirds singing every morning, I wish I could distinguish one bird from another. I identify the honking geese as they fly over the lake, and I hear the woodpecker as he raps the bark. I can see the difference between a robin and a sparrow, but I can't tell them apart by their songs.

My husband Dan can identify the voices of many birds. He knows the robin's sweet song, and he is familiar with the squawking blue jay. He can even point out the mimicking mockingbird. So I'm trying to learn a few voice recognition tips from him.

I struggle with the same issue in my spiritual life at times. Is this the voice of conviction or condemnation? Will I let faith lead me, or will I be confused and distracted by fear? Does this voice speak life or death to my heart? Does it give me direction or cause me to dwell on the impossible mistakes of the past?

Distractions

What distracts you from hearing God's Voice?

In her book *Letting Go of Worry*, author Linda Mintle reminds us, "There is a great difference between worry and concern."[17] A worried person sees a problem, and a concerned person solves a problem. She explains, "In a word, worry looks backward and revisits failure and looks forward and assumes the worse."

At times, I become so focused on the worrisome distractions around me that I forget about the power of prayer and praise.

But what if you don't actually believe that you can hear God's voice?

God's Word promises, "My sheep listen to my voice; I know them, and they follow me. I give them eternal life, and they shall never perish; no one will snatch them out of my hand" (John 10:27–28 NIV).

In the grip of a crisis, sometimes it's hard to hear God's voice. My emotions often cause me to lose hope, especially when I can't see how something can work out. My logic and my feelings tend to resist the truth that I see in God's Word.

So what if you really don't want to pray about something?

When my kids avoided talking or listening to me, I suspected trouble would follow—a bad report card, hurt feelings, or mischief. But with the help of prayer and wisdom, I always found I was able to coax them to communicate with me.

Similarly, I also tend to pull away from God at times. But he always gives a warning sign—an emotional red flag—to reveal my need for his guidance. For instance, when I lose my sense of peace, I worry about everything.

But the Bible reminds us to seek God when we're worried. "Search me, God, and know my heart; test me and know my anxious thoughts. See if there is any offensive way in me" (Ps. 139:23–24 NIV).

As I recognize the red flag warnings of worry and anxiety in my life, I need to focus on God's Word so I can listen for his truth and apply it to my life.

I'm still not an expert on identifying the songbirds by listening to their sounds, even though I can recognize them if I can catch a glimpse of them. Yet in my spirit I know that I'm hearing a symphony of praise to our Creator.

Psalm 150:6 says, "Let every living, breathing creature praise GOD! Hallelujah!" (*The Message*).

Don't Ask Questions

Sometimes it's hard to not ask questions and just listen. But at times that is what we need to do, simply because we can't listen while we're talking.

Any parent or teacher knows this is true. One of the most frustrating challenges for teachers is to encounter students who cannot keep their mouths shut. Not only do these students fail to listen; they are disturbing everyone around them.

God wants to help us, but he will not intervene where he is not invited. Nor will he interrupt if you are talking.

Listening can be a huge challenge for me. I struggle with the impulse to interrupt others before they have completed a thought. Or even if I can resist the urge to interrupt, I often find myself thinking about what I want to say next instead of listening.

If we're dwelling on our worries, we're not listening either. We must get rid of all other distractions to be able to hear the Lord. And we need to be actively listening—keeping our ears open for his guidance.

This reminds me of how I used to turn on the baby monitor to be sure I heard my children while they were in the other room.

Similarly, I must "turn on" my ability to listen by being quiet and waiting for God to lead me. He knows my needs.

Giving Our Attention

"Are you listening to me?"

Has anyone ever asked you that question? Or have you ever asked someone else that question? Maybe that thought pierced your heart when you felt the sting of someone else ignoring or rejecting you.

When you share something from your heart, how does it make you feel when the person that you're confiding in is not listening?

Although I have been offended by this behavior, I must confess that I have been guilty of tuning out a friend or family member to focus on my phone or computer. I still struggle with listening, even though it really annoys me to be on the other end of it.

So how are your listening skills?

Working as a writing instructor has helped develop my listening skills because it's hard to really hear someone's story if you don't listen.

When someone comes to us exhausted and troubled, sometimes it's difficult to listen without interrupting. I struggle with impatience and interrupting others, especially when I think I know what is about to be said.

I'm also tempted to respond to others by interjecting my own problems or even one-upping someone else instead of listening (e.g., "Well, you think *you* had a bad day—let me tell you about mine!").

Pay Attention

The apostles returned to Jesus from their ministry tour and told him all they had done and taught. Then Jesus said, "Let's go off by ourselves to a quiet place and rest awhile." He said this because there were so many people coming and going that Jesus and his apostles didn't even have time to eat. (Mark 6:30–31 NLT)

In this passage, we see the disciples returning to Jesus after they finished their ministry assignment. The passage says that they told him "all they had done and taught."

Jesus exemplifies a wise counselor who listens. Many times, people who come to us for help just need for us to listen without comment.

James, the brother of Jesus, also addressed the importance of listening in a letter to believers who were scattered abroad and being influenced by other cultures:

> Understand this, my dear brothers and sisters: You must all be quick to listen, slow to speak, and slow to get angry. Human anger does not produce the righteousness God desires. So get rid of all the filth and evil in your lives, and humbly accept the word God has planted in your hearts, for it has the power to save your souls.
>
> But don't just listen to God's word. You must do what it says. Otherwise, you are only fooling yourselves. For if you listen to the word and don't obey, it is like glancing at your face in a mirror. You see yourself, walk away, and forget what you look like. But if you look carefully into the perfect law that sets you free, and if you do what it says and don't forget what you heard, then God will bless you for doing it.
>
> If you claim to be religious but don't control your tongue, you are fooling yourself, and your religion is worthless. (James 1:19–26 NLT)

In Mark 6, we see Jesus listening to his disciples with discernment: "The apostles then rendezvoused with Jesus and reported on all that they had done and taught" (Mark 6:30 *The Message*).

But he also taught his disciples the importance of listening to him. In Matthew 11:15, Jesus asks his disciples, "Are you listening to me? Really listening?" (*The Message*).

Frankly, I avoid confiding in those who won't listen to me. When I lose eye contact with them, I know their mind has strayed to something else other than me. But as I look into the mirror of God's truth, I realize that I'm also guilty of not listening and thinking mostly of myself.

So I ask God to forgive me for hurting others by focusing on my own needs instead of theirs. And I choose to forgive others who have failed to listen to me when I needed their listening ear. In Matthew, we read this warning: "But if you refuse to forgive others, your Father will not forgive your sins" (Matt. 6:15 NLT).

Not only does Jesus listen; he discerns our needs. When his disciples came to him after a ministry trip, Jesus observed their need for solitude and rest:

> Then Jesus said, "Let's go off by ourselves to a quiet place and rest awhile." He said this because there were so many people coming and going that Jesus and his apostles didn't even have time to eat. (Mark 6:31 NLT)

Only when we really listen to others can we identify their needs and know how to respond with compassion and concern.

A friend once told me about a conflict between her young daughter and her "know-it-all" grandmother, who had a bad habit of giving unsolicited advice to everyone without listening first. In frustration, my friend's young daughter responded to her grandmother, "You think you know everything, but you don't!"

Sometimes our failure to listen before responding can provoke a negative, emotional response from those we really want to help. In fact, the Bible warns us in Proverbs, "Answering before listening is both stupid and rude" (Prov. 18:13 *The Message*).

Extend Grace

When you listen and discern the needs of someone, do you offer your advice with grace or judgment?

I refuse to be vulnerable to someone who judges or criticizes my actions. A few names and faces come to mind even as I write this. And I know I should choose to forgive them for those offenses. But I know from experience that it's hard to do the right thing when someone is heaping guilt on me. Yet often I find myself doing that very thing—responding with shame and judgment instead of offering the hope of forgiveness and restoration.

At times, I'm tempted to repeat the same words that I despise hearing myself: "I told you so!"

But is that kind of comment really helpful? Do you think others really need to hear our reminders of their failures? I beat myself up enough with my own self-condemnation; I don't need any help. And even if I discern someone's need for repentance, I try to remember to respond in kindness instead of judgment. Romans 2:4 reminds us about this:

> Don't you see how wonderfully kind, tolerant, and patient God is with you? Does this mean nothing to you? Can't you see that his kindness is intended to turn you from your sin? (NLT)

Offer Companionship

Do you know anyone who can promise you that they will always be there for you? Maybe you do have someone that has always been there when you needed something—a parent, spouse, family member, or friend. But what if they were no longer around for some reason? Who would you go to then for companionship and counsel?

As followers of Christ, we must encourage others to be dependent upon Jesus, not codependent upon us. It's easy to be caught up in the trap of codependency when we see someone in need. Even though we might discern someone's physical or emotional needs first, the most valuable thing we can offer is Jesus.

Jesus listened to his disciples, discerned their needs, and offered them wise advice and direction, not judgment. Then he also volunteered to go with them: "Come with me by yourselves to a quiet place and get some rest" (Mark 6:31 NIV).

Jesus offered his followers guidance and direction when he said, "I am the way, the truth, and the life. No one comes to the Father except through me" (John 14:6 NIV).

Jesus also promised, "I'll be with you . . . day after day after day, right up to the end of this age" (Matt 28:20 *The Message*).

Provide Understanding

Do you know anyone who seems to understand what you are going through right now? Have they survived a similar situation? Or have they been with you through your ordeal?

It's hard to find someone who totally understands your problems and your pain, unless he is walking through the circumstances with you. Even then, he can't know everything that you are thinking and feeling unless he lives inside of you, feeling your pain, listening to your thoughts, seeing the situations from your perspective.

Jesus identifies with your needs. He knows how you feel—when you're tired or hurting—because his Spirit lives in you. If you are a follower of Christ, "Don't you realize that all of you . . . are the temple of God and that the Spirit of God lives in you?" (1 Cor. 3:16 NLT).

Jesus and his disciples walked together on their journey, and he experienced the stress of the crowds and the lack of food. And he responded to his disciples "because there were so many people coming and going that Jesus and his apostles didn't even have time to eat" (Mark 6:30 NLT).

I hesitate confiding in someone who has never experienced a similar pain or need. And I find it difficult, if not impossible, to listen to unsolicited advice from someone who doesn't comprehend my circumstances.

But even if someone lives in the same household, works in the same office, or knows all the details of my life, no one really "knows me" like Jesus!

Jesus promises to listen to our problems. God's Words offers us this hope:

> Cast all your anxiety on him because he cares for you.
> (1 Pet. 5:7 NIV)

> This is the confidence we have in approaching God: that if we ask anything according to his will, he hears us. And if we know that he hears us—whatever we ask—we know that we have what we asked of him. (1 John 5:14–15 NIV)

Are you exhausted from life's circumstances? Jesus offered to guide his disciples to find rest. Do you need to find a place of solitude, quiet, and rest?

Next, we will consider Lamentations 3:29—"Wait for hope to appear" (*The Message*).

I know you're excited to learn more about "waiting." Or maybe you've experienced enough waiting for a lifetime. But I hope you'll read on.

chapter

14

Wait

Holding onto Hope

Wait for hope to appear. (Lam. 3:29 The Message)

My son Adam and his wife Jenni struggled with many doubts during their journey to parenthood, but we held on to the hope that God had a plan for them to have children.

After five miscarriages in six years, doubt and fear continued to try to dim the flames of their hopes of having a child. But the embers of God's promises kept the fire of their faith alive.

As I focused on Adam and Jenni, I prayed, *Lord, You promise in Philippians 4:19 to provide for all our needs. And your Word also promises that You know "exactly what [we] need even before [we] ask"* (Matt. 6:8 NLT).

Soon after my prayer, I learned of a sixth conception. The next tedious waiting period ensued, and we shared our hope and support, choosing to ignore our fear of another loss.

Zechariah's Promise

As I continued to pray for our children and our grandchild, I read about another couple, Zechariah and Elizabeth, who asked God for a baby. And an angel told Zechariah:

> Don't be afraid, Zechariah! God has heard your prayer.
> Your wife, Elizabeth, will give you a son, and you are to
> name him John. You will have great joy and gladness,
> and many will rejoice at his birth. (Luke 1:13–14 NLT)

At first, Zechariah questioned this promise, so he was silenced until after the child was born because of his unbelief:

> Then the angel said, "I am Gabriel! I stand in the very
> presence of God. It was he who sent me to bring you
> this good news! But now, since you didn't believe what
> I said, you will be silent and unable to speak until the
> child is born. For my words will certainly be fulfilled at
> the proper time." (Luke 1:19–20 NLT)

But Elizabeth, his wife, did become pregnant, and she acknowledged, "The Lord has done this for me" (Luke 1:25 NIV).

After the birth of their son, Elizabeth obeyed the words spoken to her, even though others insisted she name him after his father Zechariah. "But Elizabeth said, 'No, he is to be called John!'" (Luke 1:60 NLT).

When Zechariah affirmed this chosen name, another promise was fulfilled:

> Instantly Zechariah could speak again, and he began
> praising God.
>
> Awe fell upon the whole neighborhood, and the
> news of what had happened spread throughout the
> Judean hills. Everyone who heard about it reflected on

these events and asked, "What will this child turn out to be?" For the hand of the Lord was surely upon him in a special way. (Luke 1:64–66 NLT)

This story encouraged us with the promise of God's faithfulness. And even though fear and unbelief still threatened our peace, the light of God's Word reminded us of his promises, dispelling our fear of the unknown days ahead.

Remembrance of the Lord

Jenni set her alarm for the two injections her doctor prescribed every day, determined to carry this baby full term—and weeks turned into months. They hired a carpenter to expand their small two-bedroom house to make room for the child God had promised them.

A blue and green nursery emerged after Jenni's ultrasound image revealed the identity of their firstborn—a boy. A pale blue blanket hung over the end of his crib, embroidered across one corner in dark blue stitching with his chosen name—Zachary, which means "remembrance of the Lord."

As a testimony of God's faithfulness, Jenni displayed five words with scripture promises on the nursery wall—faith, hope, love, joy, and peace—representing God's healing promises for each child they had lost on their journey.

Little Zach arrived on schedule with strong lungs and a wrinkled brow. Most people overlooked Zach's miraculous entry into our troubled world. But those who attended this birth event celebrated God's intervention over the previous nine months. We all sensed God's faithful hand on this young family. And Zach's squinted eyes peeked to see a dozen faces with smiles and tears—loved ones who had fervently prayed for him.

Another Blessing

A few years later, a popular song in the early seventies by Roberta Flack, "The First Time Ever I Saw Your Face," came to mind as the ultrasound zoomed in on the image of my granddaughter's angelic face just five days before her birth. What a thrill to experience this sacred moment, observing my granddaughter's face still in her mother's womb.

I recalled the scripture where the psalmist rested in his belief that his heavenly Father knew him even before he was born:

> For you created my inmost being; you knit me together
> in my mother's womb . . . My frame was not hidden
> from you when I was made in the secret place . . . Your
> eyes saw my unformed body. (Ps. 139:13–16 NIV)

On the day we welcomed Zach's sister, Jill, into our family, I remembered the profile of her face as it appeared on the ultrasound screen.

I tiptoed up to the stainless steel table that held her, and I watched as the nurse examined every inch of her body—from her curly brown hair to the tips of her tiny, delicate toes. A bright heat lamp beamed down on her body, and Jill shivered and squealed as she adjusted to her new environment.

Psalm 139:16 also promises that God ordered all our days and wrote them down in his "book before one of them came to be" (NIV).

Could it be that God appointed the very moments for these expectant parents to hold their precious daughter Jill and her older brother Zach in their arms for the first time?

All eyes focused on Jill's every move, but my eyes focused in on her face. In that moment, my memories of the black and white image on the ultrasound screen burst into life in full color, desperately crying out for breath, needing the waiting mother and father who had eagerly anticipated her arrival. Their promised child had arrived, and we welcomed her with open arms and grateful hearts. I sang in prayer:

> *Lord, I asked you for a miracle, but did I truly believe.*
> *That you're still a God of miracles, and I would soon receive*
> *A miracle of miracles sent down just for me?*
> *Now I believe in miracles—for a miracle, I did see![18]*

Watching and Waiting

Waiting rooms can bring out the worst in me. Long periods of waiting produce all kinds of emotional red flags—from impatience and worry to full-blown panic attacks.

Reminders of past pain, traumas, and personal losses make our current trouble seem intolerable. The dark clouds roll in, and we ignore the light of spiritual truth.

I've been assigned to many waiting rooms, especially this past decade. And I don't really like to wait; I'm very impatient for good news to arrive. But waiting does not have to be hopeless. We can find hope and resist worry when we know that God is listening to our cries for help.

The psalmist speaks of "waiting" in Psalm 40, and I particularly resonate with this line from *The Message*:

> I waited and waited and waited for God. At last he
> looked; finally he listened. He lifted me out of the
> ditch, pulled me from deep mud. He stood me up on
> a solid rock to make sure I wouldn't slip. (Ps. 40:1–2
> *The Message*)

Jumping from one waiting room to the next—crisis after crisis—and trying to help others in their time of need, well-meaning supporters encouraged me to find relief from my stress, anxiety, and exhaustion.

When I asked for advice how to obtain their suggested rest, some offered me quick fixes and temporary solutions. But nothing provided the peace that I desperately needed until I leaned on God's Word for help.

Waiting Room Reactions

If we examine some of the waiting rooms recorded in the Bible, we will see that many of the biblical characters didn't hold up too well in their waiting rooms, either.

Are you impatient?

In Exodus 32, we see the children of Israel becoming impatient as they wait for their spiritual leader to return from the mountain of God. Instead of waiting for God's guidance, they built another god to worship:

> When the people realized that Moses was taking forever
> in coming down off the mountain, they rallied around
> Aaron and said, "Do something. Make gods for us who
> will lead us. That Moses, the man who got us out of
> Egypt—who knows what's happened to him?" (Exod.
> 32:1 *The Message*)

Are you frustrated and fearful?

We find Elijah the prophet frustrated and fearful as he hid from Jezebel's death threat. But God didn't seem surprised by Elijah's waiting room panic attack. He just listened patiently to his complaints; then he sent him to his next assignment:

> When Elijah heard it, he pulled his cloak over his face
> and went out and stood at the mouth of the cave.
>   Then a voice said to him, "What are you doing here,
> Elijah?"
>   He replied, "I have been very zealous for the
> Lord God Almighty. The Israelites have rejected your

covenant, torn down your altars, and put your prophets
to death with the sword. I am the only one left, and now
they are trying to kill me too."

The Lord said to him, "Go back the way you came,
and go to the Desert of Damascus. When you get there,
anoint Hazael king over Aram. Also, anoint Jehu son
of Nimshi king over Israel, and anoint Elisha son of
Shaphat from Abel Meholah to succeed you as prophet."
(1 Kings 19:13–16 NIV)

Are you afraid of dying?

Fearful of dying, King Hezekiah begged God to heal him. And
God gave him fifteen more years of life:

In those days Hezekiah became ill and was at the point
of death. The prophet Isaiah son of Amoz went to him
and said, "This is what the Lord says: Put your house
in order, because you are going to die; you will not
recover."

Hezekiah turned his face to the wall and prayed to
the Lord, "Remember, Lord, how I have walked before
you faithfully and with wholehearted devotion and have
done what is good in your eyes." And Hezekiah wept
bitterly.

Then the word of the Lord came to Isaiah: "Go and
tell Hezekiah, 'This is what the Lord, the God of your
father David, says: I have heard your prayer and seen
your tears; I will add fifteen years to your life. And I will
deliver you and this city from the hand of the king of
Assyria. I will defend this city.'" (Isa. 38:1–6 NIV)

Has your pride prevented you from accepting help others have
offered you?

In 2 Kings 5, Naaman initially refuses to obey the prophet Elisha's instructions because of his pride, even though he had asked Elisha to ask the Lord to heal him from a horrible skin disease:

> But when Elisha, the man of God, heard that the king of Israel had torn his clothes in dismay, he sent this message to him: "Why are you so upset? Send Naaman to me, and he will learn that there is a true prophet here in Israel."
>
> So Naaman went with his horses and chariots and waited at the door of Elisha's house. But Elisha sent a messenger out to him with this message: "Go and wash yourself seven times in the Jordan River. Then your skin will be restored, and you will be healed of your leprosy."
>
> But Naaman became angry and stalked away. "I thought he would certainly come out to meet me!" he said. "I expected him to wave his hand over the leprosy and call on the name of the LORD his God and heal me! Aren't the rivers of Damascus, the Abana and the Pharpar, better than any of the rivers of Israel? Why shouldn't I wash in them and be healed?" So Naaman turned and went away in a rage.
>
> But his officers tried to reason with him and said, "Sir, if the prophet had told you to do something very difficult, wouldn't you have done it? So you should certainly obey him when he says simply, 'Go and wash and be cured!'" So Naaman went down to the Jordan River and dipped himself seven times, as the man of God had instructed him. And his skin became as healthy as the skin of a young child, and he was healed! (2 Kings 5:8–14 NLT)

Are you desperate?

In Mark 5:35–43, we see a father fearful over his daughter's death. But Jesus responded to him, "Don't be afraid. Just have faith" (Mark 5:36 NLT).

Then, in Luke 18:35–42, a blind man begs Jesus for mercy.

> When Jesus heard him, he stopped and ordered that the man be brought to him. As the man came near, Jesus asked him, "What do you want me to do for you?"
>
> "Lord," he said, "I want to see!"
>
> And Jesus said, "All right, receive your sight! Your faith has healed you." (Luke 18:40–42 NLT)

Jesus reached out and touched all of these desperate people who needed him.

Are you ashamed of your waiting room emotions? As I've expressed throughout this book, emotions can serve as the warning signs that remind us of our need for Jesus.

The book of Mark tells the story of a desperate woman who reached out and touched Jesus, hoping for healing for her long-term health problem:

> A woman in the crowd had suffered for twelve years with constant bleeding. She had suffered a great deal from many doctors, and over the years she had spent everything she had to pay them, but she had gotten no better. In fact, she had gotten worse. She had heard about Jesus, so she came up behind him through the crowd and touched his robe. For she thought to herself, "If I can just touch his robe, I will be healed." Immediately the bleeding stopped, and she could feel in her body that she had been healed of her terrible condition.
>
> Jesus realized at once that healing power had gone out from him, so he turned around in the crowd and asked, "Who touched my robe?"

His disciples said to him, "Look at this crowd pressing around you. How can you ask, 'Who touched me?'"

But he kept on looking around to see who had done it. Then the frightened woman, trembling at the realization of what had happened to her, came and fell to her knees in front of him and told him what she had done. And he said to her, "Daughter, your faith has made you well. Go in peace. Your suffering is over." (Mark 5:25–34 NLT)

Are you begging God to deliver you from a horrible situation? Even Jesus experienced painful emotions as he waited for the soldiers in the Garden of Gethsemane:

[Jesus] said, "Sit here while I go over there to pray." He took Peter and Zebedee's two sons, James and John, and he became anguished and distressed. He told them, "My soul is crushed with grief to the point of death. Stay here and keep watch with me." (Matt. 26:36–38 NLT)

Do you want God to deliver you from your circumstances or problems?

Jesus begged his Father to spare him the pain of suffering and death:

He went on a little farther and bowed with his face to the ground, praying, "My Father! If it is possible, let this cup of suffering be taken away from me. Yet I want your will to be done, not mine." (Matt. 26:39 NLT)

Does anyone really care?

Jesus reacted with strong emotions when he observed his disciples sleeping instead of praying for him during his greatest hour of need:

Then he returned to the disciples and found them asleep. He said to Peter, "Couldn't you watch with me even one hour? Keep watch and pray, so that you will not give in to temptation. For the spirit is willing, but the body is weak!" (Matt. 26:40–41 NLT)

Yet as Jesus faced his death in the garden, he *remembered* his Father's promises to him, and he began to *exalt* his Father's will over his own during his darkest hour of his crisis. Then Jesus *surrendered* his will to the will of his Father. And he took the steps of faith needed to *trust* his Father, even though he knew it meant death on a cross. Jesus discovered the supernatural power of God's *REST* as he remembered, exalted, surrendered, and trusted his heavenly Father.

Grace for the Waiting Room

If you are in a type of waiting room of your own right now, I hope you will grant yourself some needed grace. Waiting rooms are painful, if not impossible. Loaded with trauma, they often remind us of prior, horrible experiences.

You may be fighting for your own life or for the life of someone you love. Desperate reactions are inevitable. You may be frustrated with everyone around you. You may be angry with the doctors or others involved where you are now.

You are probably exhausted—waiting takes its toll on you.

You may have people telling you, "Get some rest!"

You would give anything for a good night's sleep and a home-cooked meal. Unhealthy food can be one of the worst things about waiting rooms.

May I pray for you?

Lord, help my friend as she waits. I know you understand her needs. And I pray you will comfort her during these days. Amen.

Lost Your Sense of Direction?

When life seems overwhelming, it forces us to seek new answers and direction. And it's important to know where to look.

I'm always tempted to rely on options from the resources the world offers me, like news reports. But this dependence breeds confusion and discouragement, revealing more signs of the decline of our values and way of life.

In Matthew 24, Jesus described signs of the end times. And his disciples asked, "Tell us . . . when will this happen, and what will be the sign of your coming and of the end of the age?" (Matt. 24:3 NIV).

Jesus explained that he didn't know when the end would come—only his Father knew the answer to that question: "But about that day or hour no one knows, not even the angels in heaven, nor the Son, but only the Father" (Matt. 26:36 NIV).

He also encouraged his disciples to always be ready: "So you also must be ready, because the Son of Man will come at an hour when you do not expect him" (Matt. 26:44 NIV).

How can we "be ready"? Most of the time, I can't keep up with the pace of my life, much less worry about the future—especially these days.

Jesus offered a story to encourage his disciples to focus on the things that matter most. He described a servant who had neglected his responsibilities during his master's absence, as if he never expected him to return. But when the master returned, he held the servant responsible for his disobedience: "The master will return unannounced and unexpected, and he will cut the servant to pieces and assign him a place with the hypocrites. In that place there will be weeping and gnashing of teeth" (Matt. 24:50–51 NLT).

Facing the Truth

Once again, the mirror of God's Word forces us to look at ourselves— not to shame us but to confront us with his truth.

I ask myself, *Am I living as if he's not coming back? What responsibilities am I neglecting?*

When I regain my composure and examine God's Word, I'm reminded,

> Seek the Kingdom of God above all else, and live righteously, and he will give you everything you need. (Matt. 6:33 NLT)

I ask, *What does God require of me? Am I taking care of the things that he's entrusted to me? My home? Spouse? Children? Relationships? Work? Gifts or talents?*

As I examine Matthew 6:33–34 in *The Message*, I find the specific direction I need:

> Steep your life in God-reality, God-initiative, God-provisions. Don't worry about missing out. You'll find all your everyday human concerns will be met.
>
> Give your entire attention to what God is doing right now, and don't get worked up about what may or may not happen tomorrow. God will help you deal with whatever hard things come up when the time comes.

Practicing Our Faith

How can I focus on God's presence, guidance, and provision? Once again, I turn to God's Word for help and pray, "Jesus, help me to discern your presence, guidance, and provision. What do I need to focus on right now? Give me the courage and strength to trust you with my future and to listen and obey your Word today. Amen."

What do you need to give your attention to right now? Where do you sense God's presence, guidance, and provision in your life? And how can God's Word help us refocus our thoughts and reframe the way we react to our emotional warning signs?

Reflect

Refocus and Reframe

In repentance and rest is your salvation,
in quietness and trust is your strength. (Isa. 30:15 NIV)

Throughout my daughter's unplanned pregnancy, I wrote down many of the details of God's intervention in my life, compiling my own "book of remembrance."

Then those whose lives honored GOD got together and talked it over. GOD saw what they were doing and listened in. A book was opened in GOD's presence and minutes were taken of the meeting, with the names of the GOD-fearers written down, all the names of those who honored GOD's name. (Mal. 3:16 KJV)

Later, when Mother was dying and I lost hope, I interrupted my self-pity and desperate thoughts by revisiting my journal of faith stories.

I recalled how the aftershocks of Tara's confession threatened the framework and the foundation of my faith. As we tried to rearrange and salvage our family's lives, I had serious doubts that we could survive intact. The upheaval in our home tested everything—my marriage, children, church, and friends. I wondered if any of my relationships would endure the stress.

I became very impatient at home, at work, and even with family members hundreds of miles away. I withdrew into an isolated shell, trying to shield myself from shame and humiliation. I felt family and friends slipping away. In my anger, frustration, and depression, I kept everyone at a distance from our wounded family.

My emotions drove all my decisions. I could not depend on my logic; nothing made sense. And God seemed distant and uncaring. But I had turned away, not him. He was there each time I returned, even in my desperation. When I tried to be strong, emotionally and mentally, I declined spiritually. I felt like I was sinking fast. Fear gripped me as I accepted the inevitable consequences. I had never felt so out of control. I wondered if I would have an emotional breakdown.

I quickly skipped the denial stage of grief as I internalized what would come next. But my grief and anger multiplied.

I have always tried to steer clear of angry people, hoping to avoid confrontation and inevitable wounds I would have from their careless, offensive words. I typically would bite my tongue and walk away from arguments to keep the peace. But this time, I was the angry one. And nothing relieved my grief and anger.

It became clear that I had decided to be angry and I intended to stay that way. Tara's pregnancy occupied every corner of my world. And like a bottled cola that had been shaken, negative emotions spewed over everyone close to me. All my weaknesses bled through the ever-widening cracks with my inability to ignore problems and restore peace to my family.

I would debate and lose my temper. Then I would feel remorseful, ashamed of my behavior, but unwilling to accept responsibility for it. During this trial, our deep-seated issues surfaced, and I blamed those I cared for most. Perhaps my confidence in their unconditional love for me gave me the freedom to vent on them. Or maybe I simply did not care if I offended anyone because of my own self-pity and sense of hopelessness and loss.

The one thing that protected me from being swept away was my relationship with Christ. He was the foundation my life was based on, and I discovered he was the only one to be trusted when everything around me was falling apart.

I also discovered that nothing I did or felt was hidden from God. I sensed his disapproval with my sarcastic facial gestures when someone walked off after a heated discussion. He heard the remarks I whispered under my breath. He noticed my vengeful thoughts. God even listened to the scriptures I quoted out of context that supported my positions. Religious people have been using God's Word against each other for centuries. My own hypocrisy became evident to me as I exploited my church-birthed Bible knowledge.

Our Words

God means what he says. What he says goes. His powerful
Word is sharp as a surgeon's scalpel, cutting through everything,
whether doubt or defense, laying us open to listen and obey.
Nothing and no one is impervious to God's Word. We can't get
away from it—no matter what. (Heb. 4:12–13 The Message)

The Word of God penetrates our soul and spirit like a sharp razor. But our own words wield a power of their own when used inappropriately.

"Sticks and stones can break my bones, but words will never hurt me." This cliché is wrong! Words *can* hurt. Ask any child who has been called a name. Talk to a wife who has been sliced by her husband's sharp tongue. What about the husband who has been browbeaten by a bitter wife? And the rumors spread by a gossip can cut deep into our hearts and devastate lives.

Words can destroy! And God never intended for us to use his Word to judge or injure others. Instead, he has given it to us as a guide to peace, tranquility, and right living before him. But God's peace did not rule in my heart in those days. God's Word encourages us:

> Let the peace of Christ keep you in tune with each other, in step with each other. None of this going off and doing your own thing. And cultivate thankfulness. Let the Word of Christ—the Message—have the run of the house. Give it plenty of room in your lives. Instruct and direct one another using good common sense. And sing, sing your hearts out to God! Let every detail in your lives—words, actions, whatever—be done in the name of the Master, Jesus, thanking God the Father every step of the way. (Col. 3:15 *The Message*)

"I don't want to pray about that!" I used to joke with my friend, Sheila, about not wanting to pray about certain subjects. But I found myself responding in frustration at times, and I really did not want to pray about some issues. Yet the Bible warns us: "Today, if you hear his voice, do not harden your hearts as you did in the rebellion" (Heb. 3:15 NIV).

My closest friends knew how I needed their prayers. Some were bold and approached me. Others prayed in silence behind the scene. Friends from all over the country interceded for us while we had no idea they cared enough to pray.

When I am challenged by circumstances today, God reminds me of many lessons of faith. He wants us to hand over our disappointments to him.

Daily REST

How do we find REST during our chaotic lives?

Have you ever been tempted to run away or hide from your troubles? At times, I have resisted the urge to lock myself in a closet or take a long drive for some alone time. Now I know when that urge comes, it's time to "escape in the Spirit" instead.

"I just want to run away," I confessed to a friend. "But I don't know where to go."

My friend advised, "Escape in the Spirit, Karen."

"Do what?" I asked. But I knew what she meant. She was encouraging me to find time and make a plan to seek God.

I knew my friend was right, but I had a full-time job and an unfolding disaster at home. I spent every waking moment serving someone or trying to solve problems beyond my ability.

Plus, I blamed God for my problems. *How could he let this happen?* I'd done all I knew to follow him. And I had trusted him to protect my children. Yet, to me, it appeared that God had turned his back on us.

I knew that I should choose to seek God. But that meant admitting my unbelief. I knew that he would not fail to follow through on his promises. But I had to seek his forgiveness and let go of my emotional baggage that had surfaced as a result of my current crisis.

Even when I sought God for answers, I had moments of panic. But then I would retreat to a quiet, solitary place and pray, listen, and wait for God to restore peace and order to our lives.

I learned that seeking God during hard times is a never-ending process, and difficult times are often trailed by more problems. That is why we need to develop prayer strategies to fall back on when life issues burden us.

What do you do when life becomes too hard to handle? What strategies do you use to overcome difficulties? Where do you draw strength from to get out of bed and face the next day?

The first thing I must do is to find a place to meet with God so I can speak from my heart. And in that sacred space, alone with God, he always reveals survival strategies to help me respond to my days of trouble.

One thing is for certain—trouble will visit all of us. And in those turbulent times, we must find a way to refocus our thoughts and reframe the way we manage our lives and emotions, using all the tools we've gained while in the waiting rooms of life.

Refocus

And now . . . one final thing. Fix your thoughts on what is true, and
honorable, and right, and pure, and lovely, and admirable. Think
about things that are excellent and worthy of praise. (Phil. 4:8 NLT)

A while back, I found myself in one of those brutal, self-deprecating moods. As I arm-wrestled my depression, I listed all my troubles. And I decided to pray about how to win the battle instead of avoiding it. I knew it was a spiritual onslaught—an attack from the enemy of my soul—intent on discouraging me.

I revisited the promise of REST in Philippians 4:5–9. But this time, I focused on a different word: *lovely.* "[W]hatever is lovely . . . think about such things" (Phil. 4:8 NIV).

When I noticed the unusual word *lovely,* I wondered, *How on earth can I find something "lovely" to think about?*

I wasn't feeling "lovely," and nothing around me seemed "lovely" either. But I read the scripture over and over, questioning God's purpose in leading me to this specific verse.

I decided to work outdoors, taking my laptop to our backyard deck, hoping the fresh air and sunshine would help relieve my negative thoughts.

As I sat down to write, a rustle in the branches of our Bradford pear tree revealed two squirrels playing tag. They tumbled from the tree and scampered up the wooden fence as a large blue jay chased them from his territory. I became distracted by the wildlife and fascinated by nature's confrontations in my own backyard.

The leaves rustled in the breeze as the sun peeked through the branches, casting an array of dancing shadows. Surrounded by shades of green, I relaxed for the moment in my lawn chair before turning on my computer.

Lovely, I thought. *This is lovely!*

The word *lovely* swept in once again with the stirring breeze. In a sudden and unexpected way, calm settled on me and everything seemed right once again.

Then I thanked the Lord for my own quiet and lovely moment, bathed in the shades of summer and focused on God's Word. Later, I retreated to the peace and solitude of my office to begin my next writing project.

Word Power

When I chose to seek God and focus on REST, I found the peace I needed once again.

Yet, the more I attempted to explain how to find spiritual REST, the more difficult it seemed. *How can I define it? How can you share a spiritual concept using human words?*

I can voice what I know and share my own experience, but words will never substitute for a personal understanding of REST.

How can I lead someone to engage in spiritual warfare? The Bible clearly states that we need spiritual weapons for spiritual warfare.

When I offer earthly metaphors to describe this REST experience, they always fall short and never do it justice.

When I refer to God as my heavenly Father, my explanation fails because there are many terms used to describe fatherhood. But all dads are different—each one has his unique gifts and talents.

Yet even though my words fail me when I want to communicate truth, I know I can depend on God's Word:

There's nothing like the written Word of God for showing you the way to salvation through faith in Christ
Jesus. Every part of Scripture is God-breathed and
useful one way or another—showing us truth, exposing
our rebellion, correcting our mistakes, training us to live
God's way. Through the Word we are put together and
shaped up for the tasks God has for us. (2 Tim. 3:15–17
The Message)

When friends and family struggle with horrible events, my
words seem shallow. Mere words seem inadequate to express my
emotions.

When my sister Leslea lost her two-year-old son, Colter, in
a tragic accident, I prayed, *Lord what will they do? How can they
survive such a loss?*

What can we do when life delivers unbearable circumstances?
I can't imagine the pain—I refuse to let my thoughts go there.

Where can we go? Who do we run to? What should we cling
to when we're drowning in a sea of sorrows? Will someone throw
us a lifeline? Will we survive?

My precious nephew's death didn't mark the first time I found
myself unable to offer human words to bring peace and comfort
to a parent faced with the death of their child.

Now, after surviving many trials and crises, I know where to go.
And I know who to run to. I know who to cling to when drowning
in grief and who will throw a lifeline. And I know how to survive:

- *Help.* The Lord promises to give us his powerful Word to
  help us when we don't know what to say or pray. "[T]he
  Spirit helps us in our weakness. We do not know what we
  ought to pray for, but the Spirit himself intercedes for us
  through wordless groans" (Rom. 8:26 NIV).
- *Hope.* The Holy Spirit offers promises of hope, even if we
  never understand why these things happen. "I pray that

God, the source of hope, will fill you completely with joy and peace because you trust in him. Then you will overflow with confident hope through the power of the Holy Spirit" (Rom. 15:13 NLT).

- *Assurance.* God's Word provides the assurance that Jesus will bear our grief and carry our sorrows. "Yet it was our weaknesses he carried; it was our sorrows that weighed him down. And we thought his troubles were a punishment from God, a punishment for his own sins!" (Isa. 53:4 NLT).

- *Peace.* God's Word can speak peace to the storm ravaging our dreams. And he promises to throw us the lifeline of his Word. "Then you will experience God's peace, which exceeds anything we can understand. His peace will guard your hearts and minds as you live in Christ Jesus" (Phil. 4:7 NLT).

- *Confidence.* We can have the confidence to know that in Christ we will survive. And we can expect him to provide the power we need to overcome any circumstance in our life if we trust him with the situation. Healing and hope for the future can be found in him. "This is the confidence we have in approaching God: that if we ask anything according to his will, he hears us. And if we know that he hears us—whatever we ask—we know that we have what we asked of him" (1 John 5:14–15 NIV).

As I pray for my family and friends, God continues to guide my prayers with his Word. So I pray these promises from God's Word will give hope to you and others who suffer under the heavy burden of loss and grief.

REST from What?

God promised his people in the Old Testament a land of rest. He placed a visual image of that place in their hearts:

The Lord said, "I have indeed seen the misery of my
people in Egypt. I have heard them crying out because
of their slave drivers, and I am concerned about their
suffering. So I have come down to rescue them from the
hand of the Egyptians and to bring them up out of that
land into a good and spacious land, a land flowing with
milk and honey." (Ex. 3:7–8 NIV)

But they had no idea how to find their promised land. Then their
disobedience prevented them from crossing the final river before
them: "So God's rest is there for people to enter, but those who
first heard this good news failed to enter because they disobeyed
God" (Heb. 4:6 NLT).

They couldn't enter God's promised land of rest leaning on
their own strength and wisdom. An earthly leader could only lead
them to the river. They experienced miraculous acts of God to be
there and even more help from him to enter the new land.

Finding their promised land proved to be a day-by-day journey, just as it is for us. And we need God's strength for our next
step, too.

We cannot guarantee what only God can provide. No one can
follow an outline of steps to find spiritual REST any more than an
alcoholic can find freedom from their addiction by simply using
a twelve-step program without divine help.

I can share the *Words That Change Everything* for me. I can tell
you my story. But you must find your spiritual REST and salvation
alone; it's a personal journey. And I won't dare hint that I know the
specific road you need to follow to find REST.

The bottom line is that we all need REST daily. It's not a once-
and-for-all experience. Even right now, as I write this, I need physical, mental, emotional, and spiritual REST. I cannot store it up for
tomorrow. I must seek REST every day.

I'm reminded of the manna that God provided for the children of Israel in the wilderness. They were told to gather it every day because they couldn't collect more than they needed for the day. Consider what happened when they tried to store it:

> So Moses told them, "It's the bread GOD has given you to eat. And these are GOD's instructions: 'Gather enough for each person, about two quarts per person; gather enough for everyone in your tent.'"
>
> The People of Israel went to work and started gathering, some more, some less, but when they measured out what they had gathered, those who gathered more had no extra and those who gathered less weren't short—each person had gathered as much as was needed.
>
> Moses said to them, "Don't leave any of it until morning."
>
> But they didn't listen to Moses. A few of the men kept back some of it until morning. It got wormy and smelled bad. (Exod. 16:15–20 *The Message*)

The same is true with spiritual rest: I need it daily. I must search for it every day, and I can't store it up for tomorrow. No magic words can produce it—the words God gives must be received each day.

I pray you will seek the one who can communicate his Word to your soul. Only he can give you the Word that will help you achieve spiritual REST. Only he can guide you and heal your heart:

> When I think of all this, I fall to my knees and pray to the Father, the Creator of everything in heaven and on earth. I pray that from his glorious, unlimited resources he will empower you with inner strength through his Spirit. Then Christ will make his home in your hearts as you trust in him. Your roots will grow down into God's

love and keep you strong. And may you have the power to understand, as all God's people should, how wide, how long, how high, and how deep his love is. May you experience the love of Christ, though it is too great to understand fully. Then you will be made complete with all the fullness of life and power that comes from God.

Now all glory to God, who is able, through his mighty power at work within us, to accomplish infinitely more than we might ask or think. Glory to him in the church and in Christ Jesus through all generations forever and ever! Amen. (Eph. 3:14–21 NLT)

Reframe

Whatever you have learned or received or heard from me, or seen in me—put it into practice. And the God of peace will be with you. (Phil. 4:9 NIV)

I love to recount the lessons that matter most to me—this story is one of them.

Tara had to miss the second-grade Valentine's Day party at her school. She anticipated and planned for their class party for weeks. Her class decorated white paper sacks with red hearts and strung them along the chalkboard tray in their classroom.

She had worked on her valentines for hours, writing special notes for each of her friends. The parents were scheduled to bring candy, cupcakes, and punch, adding to the excitement for their children.

The afternoon before the party, Tara arrived home from school with a fever. Her symptoms indicated a throat infection.

"I don't want to miss my party," Tara whined as I offered her a Popsicle to soothe her throat, placing my hand on her fevered forehead.

I scheduled an appointment for Tara the next morning with our pediatrician, and I wondered how to break the news to her. When I told her that she'd have to miss the Valentine's Day party, I was surprised when she didn't respond in anger.

Instead, she voiced her hope that the doctor would help her feel better. And as we left his office, a thoughtful nurse offered Tara a small box of heart-shaped candies.

On our way home, we detoured for ice cream. Later, I also dropped Tara's valentines off at her school, and I picked up her sack of red hearts and candy. As she opened her decorated bag, she read every card. Later, she made valentines for her brother and her dad while she watched cartoons.

By the time Dan arrived home with a box of chocolates for her, Tara felt much better. And by bedtime, she seemed content.

"Did you have a good Valentine's Day?"

"It could have been worse," Tara said.

Then she told me a story that her Sunday school teacher had shared a few weeks earlier.

A young boy had fallen off his bicycle while he played with his friends and scraped his knee. When his mom asked him why he did not come inside even though he was bleeding after his fall, he responded, "It could be worse!"

Then the boy explained that he did not want a little skinned knee to ruin his day.

Tara identified with the boy's dilemma; she chose not to allow her illness to ruin her Valentine's Day.

Tara demonstrated an important truth that day—it could be worse!

Isaiah 11:6 promises that "a little child will lead [us]" (NIV).

My children have taught me a lot through the years. And Tara taught me that day the importance of reframing the way I approach negative circumstances in my life and finding a more positive way to look at life. I can always find something to be grateful for, even when things seem hopeless.

> "The rain came down, the streams rose, and the winds
> blew and beat against that house; yet it did not fall,
> because it had its foundation on the rock." (Matt. 7:25 NIV)

Lessons from a Storm

I wrote about the story of Tara telling me "It could be worse!" because it taught me to praise God no matter what my circumstances look like.

I have found her conclusion to be true—it could be worse, and it did get worse for us at times.

So what do we do when things just seem to keep stacking up against us?

God's Word gives us the direction we need. And I think the account of Paul's shipwreck in Acts 27 offers deep insight.

When Dan shared what God taught him in these passages, they became a truth that we both came back to often, especially in challenging days.

In this account, Paul has been in prison, and his newfound faith in Christ offends his Jewish brothers. Eventually they arrest him in an attempt to charge him with crimes for his beliefs. At this point during Paul's imprisonment, he is being taken by boat to be arraigned and tried as a Roman citizen before Caesar, emperor of Rome.

One seemingly contradictory fact about this story is that the Holy Spirit led Paul to Jerusalem where he was arrested. I thought, *Why would the Holy Spirit lead him into such conflict?*

> And now I am bound by the Spirit to go to Jerusalem. I
> don't know what awaits me, except that the Holy Spirit
> tells me in city after city that jail and suffering lie ahead.
> But my life is worth nothing to me unless I use it for

finishing the work assigned me by the Lord Jesus—the
work of telling others the Good News about the wonderful grace of God. (Acts 20:22–24 NLT)

During his court appearance, Paul presented the story of his conversion several times to Jewish and Roman officials. Paul would
have probably never obtained an audience with those men under
other circumstances. I've experienced similar results—as a follower
of Jesus, my troubles have led me to places I would've never gone.

Next, they placed Paul on a doomed ship during the season of
violent storms. Paul found himself in a hopeless situation, subject
to the whims of a devastating storm and ocean currents.

When all seemed lost, Paul instructed the sailors and soldiers
to employ strategies that he promised would save them all: "So
they cut off the anchors and left them in the sea. Then they lowered
the rudders, raised the foresail, and headed toward shore" (Acts
27:40 NLT).

Let's examine the four major strategies employed here:

1. *Anchors.* They cut loose the four sea anchors—used to
   steady the ship—and released them to the depths of the sea.
2. *Rudders.* They lowered the rudders—the only thing guiding their ship away from the rocks.
3. *Foresail.* They raised the foresail into hurricane force
   winds, which violates all sailing rules and would be likely
   to destroy the ship.
4. *Shore.* They headed toward the shore—the strong wind in
   the sails drove the ship toward a nearby island, and they
   focused on the direction that the ship would now take
   them.

As Dan and I examined this scripture during trying times, we
asked the Lord questions based on Paul's directives given to those
men to save their lives.

1. What are our anchors? What things in our lives do we need to release that we think are holding us steady? Jobs, money, relationships?

2. What are our rudders? What things do we insist on doing to guide us that we need to let go of? Plans, dreams, methods, opinions?

3. How can we lift our sails? Are we willing to let the Holy Spirit guide us, even when it seems we are traveling into difficult waters?

4. Where are we going, and who are our witnesses? Who will be saved in spite of the dangers the future holds?

Since Dan and I started following Jesus, we have faced one crisis after another. And we always had to examine whether we would be willing to face hardships, even if it threatened our family's well-being.

In Paul's account, not one person died in the shipwreck. But they landed in a place they never planned—the island of Malta. While there, Paul built a bonfire for warmth, and a deadly viper crawled out of the woodpile and bit his hand.

Again, just when you think Paul's problems have reached a breaking point, a deadly snake attacks him. Yet the venom from the snake didn't distract or harm Paul—which left all the witnesses there in awe.

This story offers a promise that others will know of our struggles, but it also assures us that wherever the Holy Spirit leads us, there will always be those impacted by our reactions and commitments—good and bad.

So here are my questions for you today:

1. What are your anchors?

2. What are you using for rudders?

3. How can you lift your sails?

4. What direction are you going? Who are the witnesses observing you?

Your ability to identify these things in your journey promises to help you overcome the impossibilities of your struggles and be able to see how the Lord can direct your paths as long as you trust him.

You may well emulate Paul's directions, cutting loose all worldly advice and allowing the wind of God's Spirit to lead you to a safe place—because the Lord's Word can *change everything*.

So, "[w]hen life is heavy and hard to take, go off by yourself. Enter the silence. Bow in prayer. Don't ask questions: Wait for hope to appear" (Lam. 3:28–29 *The Message*).

Then REST:

- *Remember.* The Lord is near—he promises to show you the anchors you need to release in your life.
- *Exalt.* Lift up God's Word over your circumstances and let go of your own efforts.
- *Surrender.* Lift up your white flag, allowing the Holy Spirit to guide you.
- *Trust.* Put your confidence in God to guard your heart and mind as he guides you with his peace.

Afterword

And now, dear brothers and sisters, one final thing:

Fix your thoughts on what is
true . . .
honorable . . .
right . . .
pure . . .
lovely . . .
admirable.

Think about things that are
excellent . . .
worthy of praise.

Keep putting into practice
all you learned . . .
received from me—
everything you heard from me . . .
saw me doing.

Then the God of peace will be with you.
(Phil. 4:8–9 NLT)

And thank you, Lord, for your
WORD THAT CHANGES EVERYTHING!

Now to him who is able
to do immeasurably more than all we ask or imagine,
according to his power that is at work within us,
to him be glory in the church and in Christ Jesus
throughout all generations, for ever and ever! Amen.
(Eph. 3:20–21 NIV)

Notes

[1] Karen Jordan, "Not unto Us," unpublished song.

[2] Karen Jordan, "Pour In," unpublished song.

[3] Brené Brown, "The Power of Vulnerability," TED Talk, June 2010, accessed October 19, 2015, http://www.ted.com/talks/brene_brown_on_vulnerability.

[4] Beth Moore, *So Long, Insecurity* (Carol Stream, IL: Tyndale, February 2010).

[5] Camp Fire First Texas, "A Brief History of Camp Fire First Texas," accessed July 15, 2015, http://www.campfirefw.org/about-us/history.

[6] Jack R. Taylor, *The Key to Triumphant Living* (Nashville: Broadman Press, 1971).

[7] Creitzfeldt-Jakob Disease Foundation, "CJD Fact Sheet," accessed June 30, 2015, http://www.cjdfoundation.org/cjd-fact-sheet-0.

[8] Charles Haddon Spurgeon, "Israel at the Red Sea," The Spurgeon Archive, accessed June 30, 2015, http://www.spurgeon.org/sermons/0072.htm.

[9] Philip Campbell, Carina Dennis, and Richard Gallagher, "Everyone's Genome," *Nature 409* (February 15, 2001): 813. doi:10.1038/35057264.

[10] Samuel Stennett, "On Jordan's Stormy Banks," in *Baptist Hymnal* (Nashville, TN: Convention Press, 1975), no. 490.

[11] Karen Jordan, "Who He Is," unpublished song.

[12] Karen Jordan, "Sacrifice of Praise," unpublished song.

[13] John Piper, *The Passion of Jesus Christ* (Carol Stream, IL: Crossway, 2004).

[14] Rosalind Rinker, *Prayer: Conversing with God* (Nashville: Zondervan, 1986).

[15] Peter Lord, *Hearing God* (Ada, OK: Baker, 1988).

[16] Charles Haddon Spurgeon, "Education of the Sons of God," Spurgeon Gems and Other Treasures, accessed June 30, 2015, http://www.spurgeongems.org/vols46-48/chs2722.pdf.

[17] Linda Mintle, *Letting Go of Worry* (Eugene: Harvest, 2011).

[18] Karen Jordan, "Asking for a Miracle," unpublished song.

RESTNotes

An Invitation from Karen

If you were inspired by
Words That Change Everything,
I invite you to visit my website
http://www.karenjordan.net
and sign up for my free
RESTNotes
to use as a devotional companion
to this book.

You will also find more
devotionals,
legacy stories,
and other free resources,
encouraging you to
tell the stories that matter most
and to seek spiritual peace and
REST from your worries in

God's Word—
Who Changes Everything!

About the Author

Karen Jordan encourages others to tell the stories that matter most as an author, speaker, writing instructor, and blogger, focusing on topics about her faith, family, and writing. Karen and her husband, Dan, live in Hot Springs Village, Arkansas, near their two children and seven grandchildren.

Karen addresses faith-based groups and teaches workshops for women's conferences and retreats. A former adjunct writing instructor for University of Arkansas at Little Rock (UALR), Karen also teaches writing workshops for various writers' conferences, writers' groups, community organizations, and faith-based organizations.

To read more of Karen's stories, connect with her online:
http://www.KarenJordan.net

Facebook
https://www.facebook.com/KarenBarnesJordan

Twitter @KarenJordan
https://twitter.com/KarenJordan